ALI
IN ACTION

To Muhammad Ali, not just my No. 1 sports hero, but my personal hero, whose acts of courageousness have been a lifelong inspiration.
Thanks, Champ!

ALI
IN ACTION

THE MAN, THE MOVES, THE MOUTH
LES KRANTZ

THE LYONS PRESS
Guilford, Connecticut

The Lyons Press is an imprint of
The Globe Pequot Press

Contributing Writers: Bobby Cassidy, Bill Chastain, Marty Strasen

Published in the United States
by The Globe Pequot Press
P.O. Box 480
Guilford, Connecticut 06437
United States of America
www.globepequot.com

The Lyons Press is an imprint of The Globe Pequot Press.

Cover Photo by Gordon Parks; Courtesy: Meserve-Kunhardt Foundation

All photos courtesy of AP Wideworld, except for photos from Corbis, which are on the following pages: 11, 13, 18 (bottom), 29, 36, 39, 40-41, 44, 64-65, 84, 85, 87, 93, 94, 121, 123, 125, 126-27, 128, 130, 131, 132, 147 (left), 149 (left).

Produced by: Facts That Matter, Inc.
Designed by: Julie Shimer

Library of Congress Cataloging-in-Publication Data is available on file.
ISBN 978-1-59921-302-6

Printed in Malaysia

10 9 8 7 6 5 4 3 2 1

Acknowledgments

The author wishes to thank his contributing writers as well as Bert Sugar for his fine narration of the DVD documentary and Angelo Dundee for his amazing foreword.

Thanks, too, to David Aretha, who helped edit the book and served as the principal writer of the DVD's script. It was a pleasure and privilege to work with my Lyons Press editor, Tom McCarthy, and his publisher and my good friend, Gene Brissie, who has always had an eye for innovative books and knows how to inspire.

Thanks also to the book's designer, Julie Shimer; fact-checker, Ed Maloney; and proofreader, Katherine Hinkebein. Other vital contributors to this book include film footage researcher Susan Hormuth, Sara Bower of ITN, and Jay Rizick of ESPN as well as Jerry Perenchio, Kathleen Antion, Katie Schwartz, and Don Petroni.

I am also grateful to our video editors, Jack Piantino and Kristie Back, who did such a fine job with our accompanying documentary, and our sound engineer, Bill Ebmeyer of Oakdale Post Audio in Las Vegas.

Les Krantz

ALI IN ACTION

THE MAN, THE MOVES, THE MOUTH

"Inside of a ring or out, ain't nothing wrong with going down. It's staying down that's wrong."

—Muhammad Ali

FOREWORD BY ANGELO DUNDEE

During the two-plus decades that Muhammad Ali and I were together, I was part of his wonderful love of life. The key was laughter. We always had fun, no matter how rough the situation was. He always found a way to laugh and make others around him laugh.

Let me tell you about the first time I met him. I was holed up in a Louisville hotel room with my fighter, Willie Pastrano. It was the day before a big fight, and while we were watching TV, the phone rang. I picked it up and what should I hear but a rush of words tumbling out that sounded like: "Hello, my name is Cassius Marcellus Clay and I'm the Golden Gloves champion of Louisville, I won the Atlanta Golden Gloves, I'm gonna be the Olympic champion and the champion of the world…" and on and on, the words flying by so fast that I couldn't remember then and can't now. And then he said, "I'm downstairs and want to come up and talk to you and Mr. Pastrano." And wouldn't you know it, those five minutes stretched into almost three and a half hours.

It was always like that with Ali. He could fill any space with what those who use $20 words call exuberance. Like the time he went "Bear hunting," trying to bait Sonny Liston. Or the times he clowned with everyone in the gym, like the Beatles. Or spouted poetry, some of which I helped him with, though I never could figure out how to rhyme Muhammad Ali. Or played practical jokes on his friends, some of which he played on me. He was not just the life of the party; he *was* the party.

Let me tell you about some of those practical jokes he pulled on yours truly. There was the time we were staying in adjoining rooms in a Los Angeles hotel, and he figured out a way to tie a long cord under the door that shook the blinds in my room. All night this went on. I was scared to death and never figured out what was happening. And then there was the time he put on a white sheet and jumped out of the closet in my room, scaring the bejesus out of me while he doubled over in laughter. It was always like that. Every day was a picnic. No, make that an all-you-can-eat buffet.

Over the years we spent together, we were more than just fighter and trainer. We had a special relationship. I allowed him to be who he wanted to be. I have always made it a point not to interfere with the personal life of my fighters. Ali respected me and defended me when influences in his life made it tough for him to do so. As a fighter, he could reach down inside and do things most others can't. As a man, he stood on his principles.

I'm proud to have been a friend of his. He made me rich in so many ways during the most fun years I've ever had. There has never been anyone like him and I doubt there ever will be again.

**Angelo Dundee
with Cassius
Clay, 1962.**

BIG DREAMER

CHAPTER 1

Clay *(left)* flashes a
contagious smile as
he trains with Johnny
Hampton as an up-and-
coming 17-year-old in
Miami Beach in 1959.
The following year,
Clay would become an
Olympic gold medalist.

A 12-year-old Cassius Clay, in his hometown of Louisville, Kentucky, shows off the quick hands that would go on to win an Olympic gold medal, 56 professional fights, and the world heavyweight title three times over.

Big Dreamer

Cassius was very close with his mother, Odessa, whom he said "taught us to love people and treat everybody with kindness." She worked as a household domestic to help make ends meet. His father, Cassius Sr., made his living as a painter and sang in local clubs.

In 1954, Cassius Clay, who was just 12 at the time and rail thin, went off on his new bicycle looking for adventure with Johnny Willis, his best friend. Their destination turned out to be a local recreation center where a show would be taking place. For the youngsters, the show's free hot dogs and soda served as more than ample motivation to make the scene.

Clay and his friend enjoyed themselves all afternoon, but the fun stopped when they were ready to leave. When they returned to where Clay had left his bicycle, they discovered that his pride and joy had been stolen. Clay felt a whirlwind of emotion as tears poured from his eyes. He felt broken-hearted about the loss of his bike, and he was frightened that he would get in trouble with his father. He also felt angry that someone had the audacity to steal something of his.

On the same premises as the show was a boxing gym run by a police officer. Clay was directed to the officer and, while in the man's company, Cassius talked about how he was going to find the person who stole his bike and teach him a lesson. Seizing the opportunity to bring a youth into the fold, the officer, Joe Martin, told Clay it would be best if he first learned how to fight. Shortly thereafter, the 95-pound Clay stepped inside the Columbia Gym—and the boxing world would never be the same again.

Clay was hooked. Years later he spoke about what went through his head in choosing to become a boxer.

"About the only other sport I ever thought about was football, but I didn't like it, because there was no personal publicity in it: You have to wear too much equipment and people can't see you," he said. "Folks sitting back in the bleachers can't hardly pick you out of a field of 22 men and a bunch of other guys shufflin' in and out, but in a boxing ring there's only two men. I made my decision about sports when I was a 12-year-old kid, and I went with boxing because fighters can make more money than other athletes and the sport isn't cut off by a season, like football. And I've never regretted that decision, 'cause when you're the greatest at what you're doing, how can you question it?"

Despite his slight build, Clay showed the reflexes and quickness of a kid with potential. Six weeks after taking up boxing, he stepped into the ring for his first-ever fight against a youngster named Ronnie O'Keefe. Clay won a split-decision in three rounds. Not only did he win the fight, but he received positive strokes from his father for doing so, further fueling his budding passion for the sweet science as well as his penchant for running his mouth.

"Almost from my first fights," he said, "I'd mouth off to anybody who

"When I was no more than a kid fighter, they would put me in bills because I was a drawing card, because I ran my mouth so much." —ALI

would listen about what I was going to do to whoever I was going to fight. People would go out of their way to come and see, hoping I would get beat. When I was no more than a kid fighter, they would put me in bills because I was a drawing card, because I ran my mouth so much. Other kids could battle and get all bloody and lose or win and didn't hardly nobody care."

Employing his unorthodox style, which relied on his uncanny speed, Clay progressed rapidly through the amateur ranks. Records of his triumphs and defeats are unclear, though Ali biographer Thomas Hauser calculated that he won 102 fights and lost just six. Included in the losses was a decision to Jimmy Ellis, who would later become his sparring partner and would briefly reign as heavyweight champion.

Clay won the Louisville Golden Gloves in 1958, but he lost in the semifinals of the nationals, which were held in Chicago that year. In 1959 he won his first national Golden Gloves title, as a light heavyweight, along with the AAU light-heavyweight title. The following year, Clay was the heavy favorite to again win the Golden Gloves light-heavyweight title, except he threw a wrinkle into the plans.

Instead of entering the tournament as a light heavyweight, he did so as a heavyweight to avoid any possibility of fighting his brother, Rudy. The Clay brothers each captured their respective divisions in Louisville to advance to the Golden Gloves Tournament of

Rudy Clay *(left)* helps his kid brother, Cassius, train with some medicine ball work in their hometown of Louisville in 1960. The younger Clay was training for that year's Summer Olympics in Rome.

Champions held at Chicago Stadium, where Rudy was eliminated in his second fight.

Clay fought Jimmy Jones in the finals. Jones reigned as Chicago's defending heavyweight champion, but Clay defeated him handily. The following account of the fight that took place on March 9, 1960, appeared in the *Chicago Tribune*: "Clay, as shifty and clever as any of the heavyweights who preceded him since the tournament came into being in 1928, knew Jones was dangerous, but after feeling him out in the first round, went on to win the next two without much trouble."

By winning, Clay became part of the Chicago team that advanced to the Golden Gloves finals, held on March 21, 1960, at Madison Square Garden in New York. Clay's opponent would be Gary Jawish of Washington, D.C., who worked for the NFL's Washington Redskins and greatly outweighed Clay.

A crowd of 15,295 watched Jawish try to use his sizeable weight advantage to bully Clay, but Cassius was too much of a boxer for Jawish. Early in the third round, Clay cut loose with a vicious flurry of punches to floor his foe. Moments after Jawish received a standing eight count, the match was stopped and Clay was declared the winner by a technical knockout at 1:59. He had won his second Golden Gloves title.

The 1960 Rome Olympics were just ahead, but Clay had other thoughts on his mind immediately after the fight when he told Martin: "Let's forget the Olympics. I'm ready to turn pro."

But the professional ranks would have to wait, as the Olympics indeed became the next step for Cassius Clay.

Olympic Gold

Chapter 2

Australia's Tony Madigan
absorbs a right hand
from Clay during the
light-heavyweight box-
ing semifinals in the
1960 Olympics in Rome.
The American scored a
unanimous decision in
a rematch of an earlier
amateur battle between
the two.

OLYMPIC GOLD

American boxers wound up dressed in gold at the Olympic Village in Rome in 1960. Cassius Clay, just 18, was flanked by fellow Olympic champs Wilbert McClure *(left)* and Edward Crook.

When Cassius Clay embarked for the Rome Olympics in 1960, he willingly played the role of the All-American boy. He was tall, handsome, and athletic. And while he wore the red, white, and blue with pride, he was more concerned with another color: gold.

In a few short years, Clay would galvanize a movement in the United States that would test his morality and courage and set forth a debate that raged in the highest halls of government. He would come to prominence not just as a fighter but as the social conscience of a divided nation. In Rome, however, Clay was still an earnest Olympian looking for a springboard to the lucrative world of professional boxing. And if he could make his family and country proud along the way, all the better.

A then-record 5,348 athletes from 83 nations competed at the Games of the XVII Olympiad during the summer of 1960. The Olympic Village housed an array of stars, from Rafer Johnson and Wilma Rudolph to Jerry West and Oscar Robertson. But no other athlete would have the same impact on his sport—or the world, for that matter—than the 18-year-old Clay.

In Rome, Clay was exposed to an environment in which segregation did not exist. Everyone was equal—if not athletically, then

Nashville, city of gold records, became a city of gold medals in 1961. Olympic track champions Ralph Boston *(left)* and Wilma Rudolph joined boxing champ Cassius Clay at the jukebox.

socially—inside the gates of the Olympic Village. He thrived in the atmosphere that surrounded the Games. While his personality would surely grate fans and the media later in the 1960s, he was a welcomed breath of fresh air. He was gregarious and outgoing and made friends everywhere he went. He greeted athletes from all nations and took the time to learn how to pronounce their names. He exchanged handshakes and team pins with nearly everyone he met.

It is hard to believe that this seemingly fearless young man nearly didn't make it to the Games. The young Clay had a terrible fear of flying, and after a choppy flight home from the Olympic Trials, he desperately attempted to convince the United States Olympic Committee that he should travel by boat, rather than fly with his team. Back in Louisville, he told those close to him that he would forego the Olympics and turn professional. Finally, after a long talk with his trainer, Joe Martin, he decided to board the plane for destiny.

In Rome, Clay formed a lifelong friendship with Wilma Rudolph, a former polio patient who would win three gold medals as a sprinter. One of 22 children, Rudolph couldn't walk without braces until she was nine years old. But she struck gold in the 100, 200, and the 400 X 100 relay. When the two were together inside the Olympic Village, Clay would often introduce her to people and predict great success for the two of them in Rome.

"Everybody wanted to be near him," Rudolph told *Sports Illustrated* years later. "Everybody wanted to talk to him. And he talked all the time. I always hung in the background, not knowing what he was going to say."

> "Everybody wanted to be near him. Everybody wanted to talk to him. And he talked all the time."
>
> —WILMA RUDOLPH, remembering Clay in the 1960 Summer Olympics

While other athletes were still trying to figure out the chatty young fighter, his boxing teammates were used to his routine. "Whenever he could gather attention, he would do it," said Nick Spanakos, a featherweight from Brooklyn who was also on the 1960 Olympic squad. "The whole boxing team just stayed in and rested. We didn't march in the parade, and we didn't go to the audience with the Pope. A lot of us were antisocial, if that's the proper way to put it. But not Cassius."

Despite all of his networking, Clay was considered the hardest worker on the team. "I don't know of anybody on the team who took it more seriously than he did," said Clay's Olympic roommate, Wilbert "Skeeter" McClure. "We'd walk around and he'd go up to people and shake hands with them, but he had his mind on training. He worked for that gold medal. He trained very, very hard."

Indeed, when it came to fighting, Clay was all business. He entered Rome with six Kentucky Golden Gloves titles, two National Golden Gloves championships, and two National AAU titles on his résumé. Anyone who spent even a short period of time with Clay knew this, of course, because he told everyone. If his outgoing personality was new to the world of sports, so too was his unconventional style in the ring.

Clay had incredible natural gifts, including a unique blend of speed, agility, and power. Boxing pundits said he was a heavyweight with the hand speed and reflexes of a welterweight. It was a valuable resource against opponents who were accustomed to lumbering slugfests. Rather than standing toe-to-toe, Clay employed plenty of movement. His feet were as much a part of his attack as his fists. He would glide inside, land a barrage of punches,

Winning has its rewards. Wearing his just-earned gold medal in Rome, Clay treats himself to a new pair of Italian shoes. It was rare for Clay to remove his medal, for it was a time of great American and personal pride for the fighter.

then float effortlessly away, often leaving his opponent bewildered. His detractors called his style skitterish. To others, it was likened to ballet.

"He moved a lot, which was the style I favored," said Vic Zimet, a veteran amateur boxing official who had worked in the opposite corner of Clay. "He was very stylish even as a young fighter. It was the style of the 1930s, reminiscent of the great boxer Benny Leonard. That's how I taught my boxers how to box."

Clay's speed allowed him to get away with things that mere mortal fighters could not even attempt. For example, he fought while carrying his hands at his waist, rather than upright in the traditional defensive boxing stance. He rarely ducked or slipped punches, opting instead to pull his head straight back—still in the line of fire—to avoid incoming blows. Only an athlete with outstanding reflexes and agility would be able to survive at the world-class level while using those practices.

The world was about to find out that Clay was such an athlete.

The boxing competition at the 1960 Olympic Games was loaded with talent. Five other fighters—Nino Benvenuti, Ki Soo Kim, Vicente Saldivar, Carmelo Bossi, and Sandro Lopopolo—would later go on to win professional world titles. Benvenuti and Saldivar eventually would be elected to the International Boxing Hall of Fame. McClure would become a top-ranked middleweight as a professional.

Still, whether it was his national success or his excessive talking, Clay was the focus of the boxing competition. His impressive credentials in the States made him the favorite to capture gold inside Rome's famed Pallazzo de Sport arena.

Clay cruised through his first two Olympic matches. In the opener, he knocked out Yvon Becaus of Belgium in the second round. In his next bout, he triumphed handily over the Soviet Union's Guennadiy Chatkov with a 5-0 unanimous decision. If

Poland's Zbigniew Pietrzykowski won medals in three consecutive Olympic Games, but he had to settle for silver in Rome in 1960. Though the Pole's southpaw style caused some early problems, Clay turned in a gold medal performance.

Opposite: Last in line but first in impact, Cassius Clay stands in Rome with his 1960 U.S. Olympic boxing teammates. Clay had tried to back out of the Olympics because of his fear of flying, but it turned out to be, up to that point, the greatest experience of his life.

anyone wondered whether Clay was more style than substance, this bout went a long way in setting the record straight. How good was Chatkov? He already had won a gold medal at the 1956 Olympics, defeating Giulio Rinaldi en route to that title. The vanquished Rinaldi would later go on to split a pair of fights with the great Archie Moore.

In the semifinals, Clay found himself in the ring with a familiar opponent. In the opposite corner was Anthony Madigan of Australia. Although he was from Down Under, Madigan had lived and trained in New York and won a Golden Gloves title in 1959. He and Clay fought once in a nationally televised amateur tournament, with Clay winning a hard-fought contest. When they met again at the Olympics, Madigan put forth another solid effort, but as much as he was fighting Clay, he was fighting destiny. Clay advanced to the gold-medal round with a 5-0 decision.

"I was impressed with his ability, but I always wondered about his heart," said Spanakos. "But the kid could fight. He had some tough fights in Rome. The Madigan fight was a war. Whenever Cassius was in a tough fight, he'd rise to the occasion."

If Clay was supposed to be skitterish, it was not evident in Rome. He handled each bout with the aplomb of a veteran champion.

Standing between Clay and Olympic glory was Poland's Zbigniew Pietrzykowski, who had already won a bronze medal at the 1956 Olympics. At 28, Pietrzykowski was a grown man, 10 years older than Clay. He was a southpaw, had fought more than 200 times, and had won three European amateur titles.

None of it mattered. After a slow start to the gold-medal bout, perhaps an adjustment to his foe's southpaw stance, Clay began to pick up the pace in the second round and never looked back. Clay's speed overwhelmed Pietrzykowski. The Louisville teenager outpunched and outmaneuvered his opponent. He landed punches in bunches, and by the time it was over Pietrzykowski was bloodied and beaten. Clay was awarded a 5-0 unanimous decision and the gold medal. Fellow Americans Edward Crook (middleweight) and McClure (light middleweight) also brought home gold medals.

Clay became an instant hero, not just because of the gold medal, but because this was the first Olympics televised back to the United States. CBS paid $394,000 for the rights, and Clay's gold-medal bout was televised in prime time.

The 1960 Olympics were groundbreaking in other ways as well. Ghana's Clement "Ike" Quartey became the first black

African to win an Olympic medal when he captured silver in the light-welterweight division. (His son, Ike Quartey, would win the WBA welterweight title in 1994). Later in the Games, Abebe Bikila, running barefoot, outlasted Rhadi Ben Abdesselem of Morocco in the marathon to become the first black African Olympic champion. It also would be the last time South Africa appeared in the Olympics under the apartheid regime. They would not be allowed to return until 1992, after the abandonment of apartheid and during the transition to majority rule.

Meanwhile, change was on the horizon in the United States, and Clay would play a tremendous role in fostering that change. But while still basking in the glory of his Olympic achievement, Clay was proud and patriotic. He wore his gold medal everywhere—to the cafeteria, to the closing ceremonies, and even on the flight home.

During an interview after his gold-medal bout, a reporter from the Soviet Union asked how it felt to earn an Olympic championship for the United States while there were still restaurants back home that refused to serve him because of the color of his skin. "Tell your readers we got qualified people

> "To me, the USA is the best country in the world, including yours."
>
> —CLAY, to a Soviet reporter in 1960

working on that problem, and I'm not worried about the outcome," he said. "To me, the USA is the best country in the world, including yours."

Much has been written about the gold medal that never seemed to leave Clay's person. He was still wearing it during a media swing through New York after the Olympic Games and throughout a 25-car victory parade in Louisville. But it vanished soon after.

In a 1992 *Sports Illustrated* story, it was reported that the medal was simply lost. But another, more popular story, told by Clay in a 1975 biography—perhaps for dramatic effect—is that the medal is at the bottom of the Ohio River. The tale goes that Clay and a friend were denied service in a restaurant near Louisville because of the color of their skin. After a confrontation with a motorcycle gang upon their departure from the restaurant, Clay was so disgusted by the treatment that he tossed the medal off the side of a bridge and into the river.

If true, the words posed by the Soviet journalist must have echoed inside his head, hurting him worse than any punches he absorbed in Rome. Perhaps they stoked a fire inside him—one that would burn for more than a decade.

A Meteoric Rise

Chapter 3

Trainer Angelo Dundee
helps his fighter prepare
for a bout with Don Warner
in February 1962. The
hard work paid off when
Clay, who had predicted
he would win the heavy-
weight title before turning
21, scored a fourth-round
knockout of Warner.

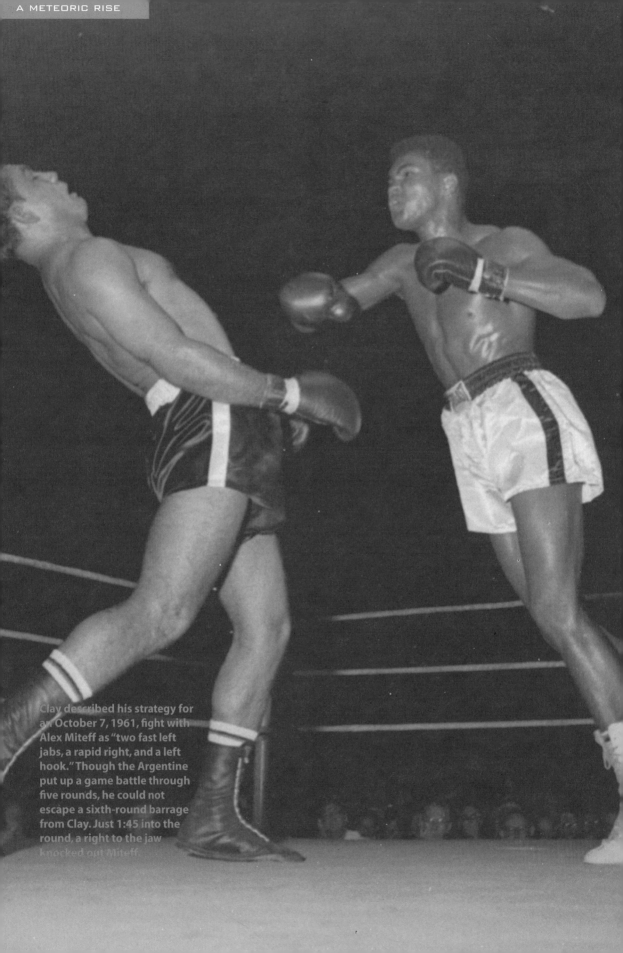

Clay described his strategy for an October 7, 1961, fight with Alex Miteff as "two fast left jabs, a rapid right, and a left hook." Though the Argentine put up a game battle through five rounds, he could not escape a sixth-round barrage from Clay. Just 1:45 into the round, a right to the jaw knocked out Miteff.

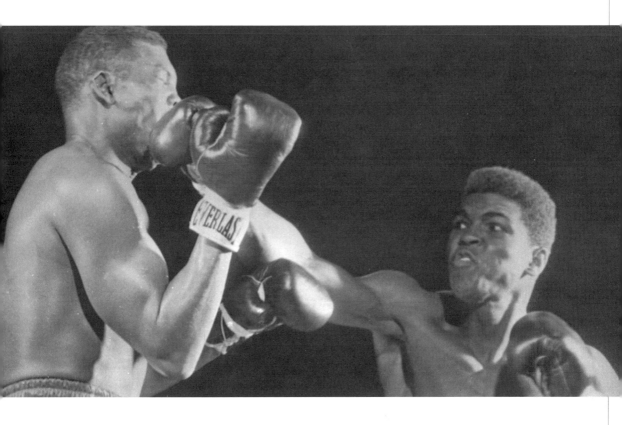

A METEORIC RISE

Don Warner's mug was no match for the right hand of Clay in their February 28, 1962, bout in Miami Beach. A straight right from Clay sent his opponent through the ropes in the fourth round, and the fight was stopped soon after.

Boxing remains the only major U.S. sport that is not governed by a national body—and the only sport in which the athletes do not have the protection of a union. But at the time that Clay was about to navigate the often treacherous punch-for-pay ranks, the influence of Organized Crime was waning and optimism was reigning.

Clay had many suitors for his services when he returned from the 1960 Olympics. He elected to keep his business close to home. On the advice of his father, Clay signed with a group of 11 white Louisville businessmen for a $10,000 cash bonus and a monthly salary of $333. The Louisville Sponsoring Group, as it was known, was about to find out how vast the potential was for their prized investment.

Clay's professional debut was akin to a football homecoming game. It was a chance for a local hero to shine in front of the family and friends who had supported him throughout his amateur career. On October 29, 1960, the 18-year-old heavyweight stepped into the ring at Freedom Hall in Louisville. Standing across the ring was Tunney Hunsaker. When he wasn't moonlighting as a heavyweight, Hunsaker was the chief of police in Fayetteville, West Virginia.

Clay shows dressing room visitors a prediction he wrote before his fight with Archie Moore on November 15, 1962—a prophesy he fulfilled when he did, indeed, stop Moore in four rounds. Clay also predicted he would go on to win Sonny Liston's heavyweight title.

Archie Moore had been a professional boxer for longer than Cassius Clay had been alive when the fading legend met the rising star on November 15, 1962. Clay knew his speed and athletic ability would be too much for his older foe. This right was one of several solid blows that, as Clay predicted, ended the one-sided bout in the fourth round.

Hunsaker could fight a little, and he must have been particularly menacing to the random Fayetteville criminal. But he was no match for Clay. Despite 17 wins in 25 pro fights, Hunsaker had never fought anyone with the talent and grace of his young opponent. Clay cruised to a unanimous decision over six rounds.

Though his talent was unquestioned, Clay still needed to find the right man to make him a better fighter. After training with Fred Stoner for his debut bout, Cassius was sent to California to work under the tutelage of future Hall of Famer—and, ironically, future opponent—Archie Moore. After a month at Moore's training camp in San Diego, Clay grew disenchanted with Moore's request to help with chores and other tasks around the camp. In December 1960, Clay returned to Louisville for the holidays. He never did return to Moore's training camp.

The Sponsoring Group considered several other trainers before finally settling on Angelo Dundee, an affable boxing lifer who had learned his trade during the sport's Golden Age. Dundee had worked as an apprentice for such legendary trainers as Ray Arcel, Chickie Ferrara, and Charlie Goldman at Stillman's Gym in New York City. By the early 1960s, Dundee had relocated to Florida and watched over a bustling stable of pugs at Miami's Fifth Street Gymnasium.

After impressing members of the Sponsoring Group during an interview, Dundee was assigned the task of steering the group's high-performance vehicle to the top of the boxing world. Dundee and management decided to wait until the new year to fight again. Clay, though, was anxious to return to the ring. He immediately set out for Miami, and as he climbed the steps of the Fifth Street Gym that very first time, he was walking straight into history. After only eight days with Dundee, Clay fought Herb Siler and knocked him out to win his second professional bout.

"I trained Muhammad in a different way," said Dundee. "I couldn't train him by the numbers. It was a completely different study with Muhammad. Boxing is a sport of individuals, and he was an individual. He had to be the innovator. I never made him feel like he was taking orders. I'd say to him, 'That was perfect the way you threw that left hook. You had your shoulder into it and you pivoted on your toe. It was perfect.' And even if he didn't throw it that way at that moment, he'd throw it that way the next time he did it."

With Dundee in his corner, Clay's career began to accelerate. He fought three times from January 17 to February 21, a span of 35 days, knocking out Tony Esperti, Jim Robinson, and Donnie Fleeman. Each bout took place in Miami Beach.

In 1960 Miami Beach ranked among the world's greatest vacation destinations. It boasted fine restaurants, glitzy hotels, and hip nightclubs. It was where the famous went to unwind. Miami Beach is located a mile across Biscayne Bay from the city of Miami. Inside Miami proper, Clay lived in the Overtown section, a small, bustling neighborhood comprised predominantly of African Americans. At the time, it was to Miami as Harlem was to Manhattan. Every day, Clay jogged five miles across a causeway from his apartment to the gym. Sometimes, he would even jog back after his boxing workout.

"The Fifth Street Gym in Miami had the same pull and mystique as Stillman's," said Dundee. "It was Stillman's at its southernmost point. Plenty of great fighters trained there, and Muhammad was always watching, always learning. He was a great student of styles. He could imitate any style."

It is often the job of a fight manager to select an opponent who offers the greatest reward while exposing his fighter to the smallest risk. Clever matchmaking can be achieved for only so long.

By the fall of 1961, Clay had improved to 8-0, and it was time for him and Dundee to take a risk. This came in the form of Argentine heavyweight Alex Miteff, a banger who had been ranked in and around the heavyweight division's Top 10 since 1957. The Miteff fight would be promoted by Madison Square Garden and televised as part of the Gillette Cavalcade of Sports series, which aired every Friday night. It was scheduled for 10 rounds.

In the buildup to the event, Clay told reporters, "My plan for fighting Alex Miteff is two fast left jabs, a rapid right, and a left hook. And if he's still standing and the referee isn't holding him up, I'm gonna run."

It figured to be a competitive match because of the two men's contrasting styles. Clay liked to stick and move, while Miteff bobbed his way in and banged away. The fight took place on October 7, 1961, at Louisville's Freedom Hall. It was Clay's third appearance in Louisville since relocating to Miami.

"My manager didn't care much for me," said Miteff. "I fought everyone in their hometown, so I didn't think much about fighting Cassius Clay in Louisville. I didn't know much about him at the time. He smiled a lot, that I remember. He was a very nice person."

Miteff was 26 years old and once the heavyweight amateur champion of Argentina. His professional résumé included a draw with George Chuvalo and victories over Nino Valdes and Willi Besmanoff. There were two characteristics that made Miteff a dangerous opponent for a young fighter. He could punch and he could take a punch.

Miteff gave Clay a good fight, and after five rounds it was relatively even. But then it was over. Clay knocked him out with a single, devastating right hand to the jaw.

"I don't remember the knockout," said Miteff. "What made him different from the other heavyweights that I fought was that he was very tall and very cool in the ring. He was a good boxer. He'd hit you, boom-boom-boom-boom, and he'd move around the ring. He did a lot of things wrong, or they were considered wrong back then. Because of that, I never thought he'd become a great success."

Back in Overtown, Clay was befriended by several members of the Fruit of Islam and was invited to attend prayers at a nearby mosque. It was in Florida that the seeds for his religious conversion and name change were planted. That would be a controversy for another day. Next on the agenda was a journeyman named Willi Besmanoff, and the man soon to be known as the "Louisville Lip" was courting his first negative publicity. Clay's confidence was soaring after dismantling Miteff, and he told a horde of reporters that he wasn't too excited about fighting Besmanoff.

"I'm embarrassed to get into the ring with this unrated duck," he said. "I'm ready for top contenders like Patterson and Sonny Liston. Besmanoff must fall in seven."

Not even the most successful fighters in history predicted the round in which their opponent would fall. That Clay, a veteran of exactly nine pro fights, had the audacity to make such a claim rankled the boxing establishment. But as Clay would say over and over throughout his career, "It ain't bragging if you can back it up."

He would indeed back it up. While it seemed Clay could have stopped Besmanoff almost at will—in fact, Dundee urged him to stop playing and end the fight early—young Cassius waited until the seventh round before calmly knocking out the 29-year-old German.

The 1962 campaign began with a string of impressive wins. Although Sonny Banks was the first man to floor Clay, he was counted out in Round 4. Don Warner, George Logan, the unbeaten Billy Daniels, and Alejandro Lavorante were all knocked out as Clay looked to punctuate the close of the year by making a statement.

Can anyone say "Archie Moore"?

For the first time in Clay's career, the media buildup to his fight garnered national attention. The two fighters traded barbs in a war of words uncommon for sporting events at the time. Clay embraced the attention and said, "Moore claims to have a Lip Buttoner punch. I have a Pension Punch. I will make

> "I'm embarrassed to get into the ring with this unrated duck…. Besmanoff must fall in seven." —CLAY

him see the light and retire."

He also made a more bold prediction to the press: "I'll say it again, I've said it before, Archie Moore will fall in four."

The fight took place on November 15, 1962, before 16,000 fans at the Los Angeles Memorial Sports Arena. While Moore was finally presented with the chance to teach his former pupil a painful lesson, it was Clay who had all the answers.

Moore, a month shy of 49, was a veteran of more than 200 pro fights. The 20-year-old Clay was climbing into the ring for the 16th time as a professional. Nonetheless, he dropped Moore three times in Round 4 and the bout was stopped.

Clay continued his ascent, and continued to line up meaningful opponents. The next challenge came from Doug Jones, who owned a 21-1-3 record and had knocked out such world-class fighters as Bobo Olson, Bob Foster, and Zora Folley.

Once again, a media buzz followed Clay to New York for the fight. A portion of the public welcomed his energy and style while the rest did not. You either showed up to see him shine or showed up to see him fall. Either way, when Clay fought, people showed up. The fight took place on March 13, 1963, before a sold-out Madison Square Garden.

In the moments leading to the first bell, Clay confidently bounced on his toes, staring across the ring at his most dangerous opponent to date. But hadn't the experts said that about Miteff and Moore? How could Doug Jones be any different?

Jones was different. He was a technically proficient fighter in the prime of his career. And he was highly insulted that Clay had predicted to knock him out in the fourth round. In the opening seconds of the fight, Jones delivered a hard right hand that momentarily wobbled Clay. The Golden Boy was in a fight, and as he walked slowly back to his corner, for the very first time, there was a look in Clay's eyes that suggested he knew it.

When the fourth round passed and Jones was still standing, the crowd at the Garden jeered Clay. The momentum was building for the New Yorker, but Clay responded with the kind of mettle that would define his career. He did not fold. Instead, Clay boxed nimbly, earnestly peppering Jones with jabs and combinations. Jones seemed to have Clay stunned in Rounds 8 and 9, but Cassius continued to use his jab to pile up points.

The Garden fell silent as ring announcer Johnnie Addie read the decision. The scoring by rounds was 8-1-1 from the referee and 5-4-1 from the two judges—all for Clay.

"That was one of the worst decisions I was ever associated with," said Jones' manager, Rollie Hackmer. "Jones gave him a boxing lesson. Jones was countering his slapping jab. He'd catch the jab and counter with a right. Anybody that fought Clay had to be able to bob and weave and counter-punch. Jones was a master at both."

The crowd agreed, chanting, "Fix! Fix! Fix!" The result will forever remain disputed, but there was no disputing the bout's significance. It proved that Clay was equal parts substance and style. The win launched him into the top of the heavyweight division's ratings.

Three months after the Jones fight, Clay traveled to London for a June 18 bout against British heavyweight champion Henry Cooper. This time, Clay predicted a fifth-round knockout. It appeared from the opening bell that Clay would have no trouble making good on his words. Cooper was getting outclassed and was bleeding badly from a cut above his left eye when, out of nowhere—boom!—he caught Clay with a left hook and dropped him in the waning moments of the fourth round. For the first time in his pro career, Clay was seriously hurt.

That's when Dundee first worked his magic with his young boxer.

"I noticed early that there was a small tear in the glove," said Dundee. "Muhammad was handling Cooper, then he got hit with that hellacious left hook. I was looking for a little time. So I put my finger into the tear and lifted it up. I pointed it out to the referee, and they needed to get new gloves."

The ploy gave Clay several minutes to regain his senses. "I told the guys in the corner, pour water over his head," Dundee said. "We got him loose as a goose again. The rest is history."

Yes it was. When the fighting resumed, Clay emerged from the corner and battered Cooper for two minutes until the referee stopped the fight. Clay prevailed in the fifth round—just as he had predicted.

Clay had predicted a fourth-round knockout of Doug Jones at Madison Square Garden on March 13, 1963. When Jones proved to be a skilled and durable foe, Cassius altered his approach, using a steady stream of jabs and this uppercut in the 10th round to earn a unanimous decision.

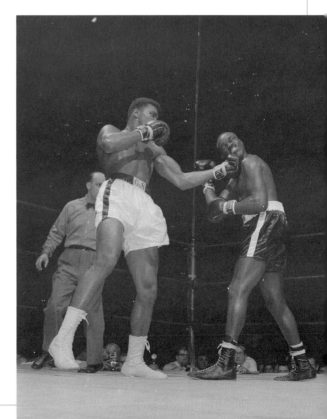

SHOCKING THE WORLD

CHAPTER 4

To no one's surprise, Clay had plenty to say after winning the heavyweight title from Liston in February 1964. His handlers held him back physically in the Miami Beach ring, but there was no stopping his mouth. The new champ declared, "Eat your words!" and "I am the greatest!"

SHOCKING THE WORLD

Clay seemed to be trying to show Sonny Liston he was crazy in the days leading up to their 1964 title bout. On February 19 in Surfside, Florida, Clay extended his fist to show a crowd of fans how he planned to punish the heavyweight champion.

Few—if anybody at all—understood Cassius Clay. Sports figures of the early 1960s were cut from a different fabric than the brash boxer. Was he a prophet, a clown, or just plain crazy?

Clay chose crazy for hunting bear.

In the summer of 1963, Sonny Liston held the heavyweight championship, the title Clay coveted. So he decided he had to be aggressive to draw out the intimidating pugilist known as "The Bear," a man whose disadvantaged upbringing had put him on a wayward path.

Liston grew up in extreme poverty in Arkansas as the youngest of 25 children. With nowhere to go, he turned to crime, which led to a five-year prison sentence for robbery. While incarcerated, Liston learned to box.

Liston displayed loads of talent in the ring. Among his physical gifts were extraordinarily large fists, believed to be the largest ever to fill the gloves of a heavyweight champion. The large mitts served him well, adding conviction to the starch-filled jab and devastating left hook—his most effective weapons in the ring. Liston's menacing looks and prison background added to his mystique. He intimidated every man in the gym, especially his opponents.

LISTON		CLAY
31	AGE	23
212	WEIGHT	210
	HEIGHT	
6 ft. 1 in.		6 ft. 3 in.
	REACH	
84 in.		79 in.
	CHEST NORMAL	
44 in.		43 in
	CHEST EXPANDED	
46 ½ in.		45 in.
	WAIST	
33 in.		34 in.
	FOREARM	
14 ½ in.		13 ½ in.
	FIST	
15 ½ in.		13 in.
	NECK	
17 ½ in.		17 ¾ in.
	BICEPS	
17 ½ in.		16 in.

The "tale of the tape" gave the younger Clay a height advantage over Liston, but the champ had the edge in reach and mass. What could not be measured on this chart were the speed, skill, and resolve of Clay, who—as usual—had predicted an early knockout.

Yet Liston showed indifference about defending his title against Clay. Not until the boisterous challenger decided to take the unorthodox tact of goading the champ did Liston finally relent.

First, Clay showed up at Liston's training headquarters while Sonny trained for his second title defense against Floyd Patterson. Clay taunted Liston during his sparring exhibitions, calling him a "flat-footed bear" while posing his quandary of whether he should "beat him or cage him." Later he appeared at the Patterson fight, which Liston won in the first round, and declared, "Liston is a tramp. I'm the champ."

Perhaps the incident that sent Liston over the edge was when Clay—after notifying Denver television and radio stations—rode a bus into Liston's neighborhood. On the side of the bus was painted "World's Most Colorful Fighter." Clay and company honked the horn and screamed out various insults. Eventually, Liston barked back at Clay, and the police were called. Without further episode, Clay left having accomplished his mission.

On November 4, 1963, Liston signed a contract to fight Clay in Miami on February 25, 1964. Clay's tact had worked. Initially, Clay appeared to Liston as just another opponent he would destroy en route to his next payday.

Despite Clay's glittering amateur record and initial success as a professional, the hardened Liston didn't seem to regard Clay at all.

Liston began to prepare for their fight in December 1963, choosing to train in Las Vegas rather than where he lived, in Denver, due to dire weather forecasts for the mile-high city. He also didn't want to train in Miami because of Clay's presence. "I don't like to hear that loudmouth," Liston said. "If I was in Florida, I'd hear it."

Early in his training, Liston offered remarks that showed just how unconcerned he was about the challenger. "I don't think it'll go past two," Liston said. "It better not go past three."

Liston's mock concern rested on the fact that he had bet a friend a wristwatch that he would beat Clay in three rounds. But he did see Clay as an upgrade from Patterson, prompting him to step up his training.

"I'm going to train harder for Clay than I did for Patterson," Liston said. "I don't want him to catch me short. I want to catch him short."

Liston heard a great deal about Clay's quickness, which he also dismissed. "That's what they say about all of them," said Liston, who noted that after he finished with his opponent, it always "looks like I'm just a little bit faster."

Opposite: "The Greatest" mixed it up with the "Fab Four" when the Beatles—*(from left)* Paul McCartney, John Lennon, Ringo Starr, and George Harrison—absorbed a fake punch from Clay at his training camp in Miami Beach on February 18, 1964. Clay was prepping for his heavyweight championship battle against Liston.

Clay turned the weigh-in for his 1964 bout with Sonny Liston into a vocal exercise. "Float like a butterfly, sting like a bee," he taunted, along with, "Rumble, man, rumble." Liston came away from the ordeal saying Clay was "scrambled in the marbles," while Clay earned a $2,500 fine for being disruptive.

Others, such as Henry Cooper of Great Britain, did not share Liston's opinion. Cooper had been beaten badly by Clay in five rounds, which was the round Clay had predicted the fight would end.

"I'll bet Cassius Clay messes him about for nine or 10 rounds," Cooper said. "He's got a good pair of legs. This fellow's fast and he boxes from a long distance, which won't suit Liston because Liston's cumbersome. I think he'll give him a much harder fight than people think."

In late January, Liston arrived in Miami and was greeted at the airport corridor by Clay, who wore a tuxedo with a ruffled shirt while leading around a rabble of interested bystanders. Once Liston appeared, the show began.

"Come out and fight," Clay shouted. "Fight me right now. You're really afraid of me."

Eventually, Liston tired of Clay's ranting and turned toward his antagonist. But before he could do anything, his manager, Jack Nilon, and several others reeled him in.

A week later, Clay showed up at the suburban Miami Surfside Auditorium, where Liston would conduct his final weeks of training for the fight. Once again the sole purpose of Clay's visit seemed to be a deep-seated desire to show Liston that indeed he was crazy. Miami police told Clay to leave, and he did.

Liston continued to train in no-nonsense fashion, as witnessed by his sparring partner, Leotis Martin, who had to quit a session with Liston after taking a left hook to the body. Afterward, Liston continued to echo confidence, noting he had gotten himself in better shape than he had been for either fight against Patterson and that he planned to knock out Clay in five rounds.

While Liston continued to sound like he didn't think Clay had a chance, other opinions to the contrary must have slipped into Liston's consciousness. After examining both fighters for the Miami Beach boxing commission, Dr. Alexander Robbins told reporters that Clay's "physical reactions are sharper than the champion's. And he shows not the least sign of nervousness.… I was surprised at the remarkable physical development and condition of this young challenger. Remember, yesterday I had examined Liston and found him a remarkable specimen; but he is older than Clay and his reactions are not as sharp."

In what might be described in later years as a "prefight smackdown," both fighters were afforded the opportunity to exchange barbs during a news conference arranged by Theatre Network Television, Inc., which

was the company that was to produce their fight. Both fighters spoke from their respective training sites, but they could see each other by looking at TV monitors. Those asking the questions from the TNT technical center in Woodside, Queens, could not see the fighters when they asked their questions. One of the initial exchanges between the pair went as follows:

Clay: "I'm the greatest thing in all history."

Liston: "I imagine he'll be talking as he's going down."

Clay: "If you whup me, I'll crawl across the ring and kiss your feet."

Liston: "I ain't gonna wait around all night until you're able to crawl."

At one point, Clay began to rant.

"You just saw that big bear," Clay said. "Is he as rangy and pretty and fast as me?… I'm getting wilder every day. I can knock a man out backing up…. I'm gonna upset the whole world…. Hey, what camera am I on?"

When Clay came up for air, a questioner asked what he felt like being the underdog.

"At these odds, I'm a poor man's dream," Clay said.

Liston maintained a stoic, threatening posture.

> "I can knock a man out backing up…. I'm gonna upset the whole world…. Hey, what camera am I on?"
> —CLAY

"Ya know, when you have kids and they don't mind you, you have to put them in their place," Liston said. "He has to keep talking, but what'll happen to him when all those people leave him and he has to come to me?… [Rather than slug it out], I expect him to jump out of the ring."

Former heavyweight champion Joe Louis, who was in Liston's camp, offered his opinion on what Clay's wisest strategy for the fight should be.

"One, he should stay away from Liston," Louis said. "Second best, he should stay away as long as possible."

Further fodder for the beating many believed Clay would take from Liston came nine days before the fight during a sparring session at the Fifth Street Gymnasium. There, Clay's sparring partner, Cody Jones, rattled Clay with two left hooks. Jones's hook hardly packed the power of Liston's, yet Clay had shown a weakness.

But boxing pundits took note during Clay's next sparring session when he employed a "bob and weave" technique previously unseen in his bag of boxing tricks. Clay had always been criticized for his penchant of pulling away from his opponent's hooks rather than

Opposite: Clay had told reporters that his strategy against Liston was "to hit and avoid being hit." He put his plan into action with several big punches, including this straight left in the third round of their February 25, 1964, title fight in Miami Beach.

Clay's aggressive approach against Liston in February 1964 was aided when his opponent injured his left shoulder early in the fight. Clay's punches would dictate the pace of the action, right up to the point when Liston could not answer the bell for the seventh round.

ducking underneath, which was believed to be the smart way to avoid a hook.

When asked about his new move, Clay told reporters: "I've got a lot of other things that neither the public nor Liston's spies have seen yet."

Reporters had a field day when the Beatles showed up to watch Clay work out at the Fifth Street Gymnasium. The boxer understood the magnitude of having the most popular music group in the world on hand, and he hammed it up accordingly.

"Hello there, Beatles," Clay said. "We ought to do some road shows together. We'll get rich."

Clay and the Beatles mixed it up in the ring in spoof-filled fashion. Photographers snapped pictures of Clay "knocking out" John, Paul, George, and Ringo all at once. Afterward, Cassius offered one of his poems about the day's events to reporters:

When Sonny Liston picks up the papers and sees,
That the Beatles came to see me,
He will get angry and I'll knock him out in three.

That same day, Clay offered insight about his always-moving mouth and the

wisdom of promotion: "If Liston beats me, the next day I'll be on the sidewalk hollering, 'No man ever beat me twice. I'll be screaming for a rematch. Or maybe I'll quit the ring for good. I think I'm getting tired of fighting."

Several days later, Clay put away his promoting skills and took on a serious front, allowing a look into what the challenger truly believed. "It is impossible for me to lose," Clay told reporters. "It is written for me to be successful. It was a prophecy for me to be successful."

He went on to state that the fight would be the biggest upset in the history of boxing. "I'm actually tired of talking about it—I'm ready to shake up the world," Clay said. "Liston's not a champion, I am. He's got my job. He's too ugly to be champion.

"He's not even colorful. If it wasn't for me, he wouldn't be talking, even as much as he has. If it wasn't for me, he wouldn't have no fans. The whole world will be watching this fight—not just the whole country, the whole world. It's impossible for me to be beaten, and he knows it, and he's scared stiff."

Throughout his workouts leading up to the fight, Clay told reporters he planned to hit and avoid being hit, prompting the scribes to tell Clay that Eddie Machen had tried to keep away from Liston and took a

Ecstatic, Clay runs around the ring after his monumental upset of Sonny Liston on February 25, 1964. "I am the greatest!" he shouted to all. "I shocked the world!" Clay continued his self-worshiping monologue while addressing the media afterward.

The normally stoic Liston got into the spirit of things by offering reporters his own poem:

> O, Cassius, Dear Cassius,
> Go home to your Ma;
> You ain't got no chance
> Against Liston's paw.

beating. Clay did not see any similarities between the two.

"Machen was afraid," Clay said. "I don't know what it feels like to be afraid. The only thing I fear is fear itself. Look, I'm too fast for that ugly bear.

"I'm going to win and be champion, and you writers better get on the bandwagon right now. If you're voting for me, write it now. I'm keeping lists. Every day we send down to the airport and get all the papers and read all the stories. Right after the fight, I'm going to have my roll call right there in the ring. I'll take the microphone and I'll say, 'This fellow said I didn't have a chance, and this one said they shouldn't permit the fight, and so forth.'"

Despite Clay's unyielding confidence, betting lines positioned him as a solid 7-1 underdog against a fighter who seemed indestructible. Joe Louis, whose wife served as Liston's legal representative, touted the champ's virtues.

Billy Conn, the former light-heavyweight champion, also weighed in against Clay. "The first punch Liston hits him, out he goes," Conn said. "He can't fight now, and he'll never be able to fight. He hasn't the experience. The only experience he'll get with Liston is how to get killed in a hurry." Conn added that Clay had stripped the heavyweight division of its dignity by acting like a "big phony wrestler."

Clay's final theatrics before the bout came during the weigh-in on the morning of the fight. Such events were meaningless for the heavyweight division, where the weight class was unlimited. Basically they served as photo opportunities. Clay viewed the activity as yet another possibility to get into Liston's head.

Clay, wearing a jacket with "bear hunting" written on the back, proceeded to tee off on Liston one last time, offering such classics as "rumble, man, rumble" and "float like a butterfly, sting like a bee." Officials fined him $2,500 for disrupting the ceremonies and his refusal to stop his antics while Liston stood on the scales.

Clay's antics struck the intended target. Afterward, Liston offered: "I don't think this kid's all there. I think he's scrambled in the marbles." If there's one thing to fear worse than a tough opponent, it's a crazy one. Was Clay crazy? Clearly Liston thought so by the day of the fight.

> "I don't think this kid's all there. I think he's scrambled in the marbles."
>
> —SONNY LISTON, on Clay

As the moment to start the fight approached, Clay entered the ring first, shadow boxing and dancing for almost five minutes before Liston joined him. When the opening bell finally rang, Liston aggressively charged Clay, furiously looking to end the fight with one punch. Clay danced away from Liston's first-round assault, dodging wild punches and using a jab to keep Sonny from succeeding.

> "I shook up the world! I don't have a mark on my face! I'm pretty! I'm a bad man!"
>
> —CLAY, immediately after winning the Liston fight

In the second round, Clay began to effectively unleash combinations against Liston, seemingly taking charge of the fight. The third round saw Clay improve his chances when he landed a right that opened a gash on Liston's cheek.

The action seemed to reach an impasse in the fourth round, but a significant occurrence took place that almost ended the fight. Clay's eyes began to sting for some unexplained reason. His eyesight blurred, and after the round he wanted to quit the fight.

"Cut the gloves off! I can't see!" the panicked Clay shouted to his trainer, Angelo Dundee. "Leave me outta here."

Clay had gone from apparent cruise control to fighting for his life in the ring. Some believed Liston's camp had intentionally put liniment on his gloves to blind Clay. Dundee felt the stinging had been either Moncil solution, an iron-based coagulant put in Liston's cut, or the residue from what Liston's people rubbed on his shoulders between rounds.

"Either way, it got on my kid's gloves and then into both of his eyes," Dundee told the *Boston Herald*. "I stuck my pinkie in his eye and put some of the stuff in my eye, and I'll tell you, it burned like hell, but I washed his eyes out with water, threw the sponge away, and then I threw the towel away, too."

Clay was not eager to step back into the ring. Referee Barney Felix said he came "within one split second" of disqualifying Clay before the start of the fifth round.

"When the bell rang for the fifth, Clay wouldn't come out," Felix said. "He kept sitting on his stool and blinking his eyes. I yelled, 'Damn it, Clay, get out there!' If he hadn't moved in a second—and I mean one second—I had made up my mind to stop the bout and award the fight to Liston on a TKO."

Somehow, Clay managed to steer clear of Liston in the fifth round. The champ seemed to sense Clay's impairment and offered his last true attack of the fight. Three minutes passed and Clay remained on his feet, heading back to the corner ready to fight another round while his vision continued to improve. By the sixth round, Clay was his old self, landing punches and dancing to dodge anything thrown by Liston that might inflict damage. After the round, the fight was scored even on points.

Stunningly, when the bell rang to start the seventh round, Liston did not get up from the stool in his corner, and just like that Clay was declared the winner by virtue of a technical knockout. Liston said he could not continue because he threw out his left shoulder throwing a hook in the first round, and the injury had worsened to the point where he could not raise his arm.

Few in the building actually knew the fight had been called until Clay jumped up on the second ring rope in his corner and began to shout: "Eat your words." When Cassius made his way to an interview for radio, he chortled about his supremacy in the ring.

"I want everybody to bear witness," he blared. "I am the greatest! I shook up the world! I don't have a mark on my face! I'm pretty! I'm a bad man! You must listen to me! I can't be beat! My face was burning and I whupped him! I'm the prettiest thing that ever lived!… I want justice!"

The commission held up Liston's purse until a review of his injury could be made, but foul play was not discovered. Cassius Clay had indeed shocked the world, and now he ruled as the heavyweight champion.

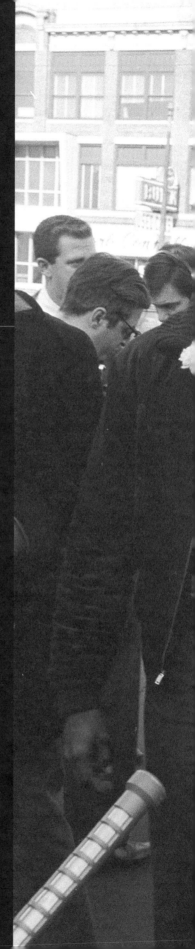

ONE-ROUND REMATCH

CHAPTER 5

One week before his scheduled rematch with Liston, the heavyweight champion stopped traffic in Boston by displaying a large rope and collar he proclaimed he would fasten around his opponent, whom he had derisively called "The Bear." Four days later, Ali needed emergency hernia surgery, causing the fight to be canceled.

Ali advised fans to arrive early for his May 25, 1965, rematch with Liston in Lewiston, Maine, predicting that the affair would not last long. Though Liston landed this body shot in the first round, it took less than a round for Ali to make good on his prediction with a knockout.

ONE-ROUND REMATCH

After defeating Sonny Liston in Miami Beach, Cassius Clay held the title as the heavyweight champion of the world. He also became Muhammad Ali. Under his new name—which was recognized by some while most continued to refer to him as Clay—the floodgates opened for a period of tumultuous times for the champ.

Ali's wife of less than a year, Sonji, was not comfortable with the religious conversion and the resulting change of lifestyle, which became a contributing factor to their eventual divorce. In addition, the Louisville Group, which had financially backed Ali, began to feel the heat to sell out—and did, to a Muslim management group.

Moreover, many still questioned the legitimacy of the first Clay-Liston fight due to its abrupt ending and Liston's criminal background. Many felt that the fight had been fixed, resulting in a climate in which none of the states with major boxing reputations wanted to sanction the rematch.

Art Laurie, the chairman of the Nevada State Boxing Commission, said that U.S. senators Kenneth Keating and Phillip Hart did not want the fight to be held in Las Vegas. "They told me not to have anything to do with that fight, because our industry here was gaming, and that fight was going to stink out the place," Laurie said.

The fight was scheduled for November 16, 1964, at the Boston Garden. Both fighters worked diligently in order to be in peak shape for the rematch. Ali's trainer, Angelo Dundee, even told reporters that he would make an offer to former heavyweight champion Floyd Patterson to serve as Ali's sparring partner for his final week of training. Patterson accepted.

"I'll even pay my own expenses to Boston as soon as he phones me to come," Patterson said. "But I won't promise not to hurt him or floor him. I'm in very good shape right now."

Liston was not impressed in the least by the news that Patterson would be in Ali's camp. The Bear, who had knocked out Patterson twice in the first round, dismissed Patterson by saying he needed sparring partners who could go more than one round. While Patterson might have been good enough to box with Clay, Liston said, "I need somebody who will give me a better workout."

Meanwhile, Ali already had begun his verbal taunting of Liston, whom Ali said he would stop in nine rounds. And if Liston got close to him, he added, he might "finish it in two rounds." "I want this to go the distance, because I want the public to get their money's worth," Ali said.

Ali even taunted Liston's advisor, Bob Nilon, who appeared at his training facility. Ali told him that he needed to "go back and tell that ugly bear" that he was as ready for him as he had been during their first encounter. He added: "I'm the prettiest. I'm the fanciest. Have you ever seen a heavyweight step like this?"

Liston trained hard and was prepared for the rematch. "I'm not making any predictions—I mean, I'm keeping that a secret for Clay," Liston said. "I think I'll come out ahead." Both fighters passed their physicals on

After performing in "Golden Boy" at the Majestic Theatre on Broadway, Sammy Davis, Jr., received some boxing tips from the champ. Ali had just signed a contract for radio rights to his 1965 rematch with Liston—a fight that would require the skills of a heavyweight rather than the voice of the popular comedian and singer, above.

November 9 and the fight, which had Liston rated as an 11-9 favorite, looked ready to come to fruition. But on November 13, Ali had to be rushed to the hospital after suffering from frequent vomiting. Once at the hospital, he had emergency hernia surgery. The fight was canceled.

Ali said the disappointment of the cancellation was worse than the pain from the hernia. He had been in the best shape of his career, and he conceded that Liston had also been in top shape. And now the fight would be delayed for however long. He could not resist taking a jab at Liston in the process when he said: "All that work for a man of his age." Liston did not take the news well, and he had an opinion on what the root of Ali's problem had been. "If he'd stop all of that hollering, he wouldn't have a hernia," Liston said.

By Christmas, Liston's conditioning had subsided to where he looked "heavier and haggard," according to a UPI report. The former champ had been jailed in Denver for investigation of drunken driving after a shoving match with 10 policemen.

In the aftermath of Liston's arrest, there was some debate about whether he would be the first fighter Ali would defend his title against. "I'd like to fight [Liston] if he'd just stay out of jail," Ali quipped. "I guess he likes the city to pay the rent."

While the status of a rematch remained in limbo, a major news event occurred that affected Ali. During a rally in Harlem on February 21, 1965, Malcolm X was assassinated. There had been a divide among the Black Muslims in which some broke from Elijah Muhammad to follow Malcolm X. Elijah Muhammad followers were believed to have been behind Malcolm X's death. Approximately seven hours after the assassination, Ali's Chicago apartment was ravaged by fire. Was this a coincidence or were the events linked? The question could not be answered, prompting beefed-up security for Ali by Black Muslim bodyguards.

A 15-round rematch with Liston eventually was scheduled for May 25, 1965, again at Boston Garden. But after an injunction was sought to block the fight in Boston, the fight was moved to Lewiston, Maine, a manufacturing city. The site of the fight would be the Central Maine Youth Center, a schoolboy hockey arena that could seat somewhere between 5,500 and 6,000. The prospect of having a small gate wasn't much of a concern to promoters, since closed-circuit TV generated most of the revenue for the fight.

Hosting the Ali-Liston rematch was about the biggest thing to ever happen to Lewiston, population 41,000, but it wasn't easy. Lewiston's police force was tripled due to the rumors that black nationalists, who were followers of Malcolm X, were going to try to kill Ali.

Ali wrapped up his training three days before the fight and spoke to reporters about where he stood with a simple "I'm getting strong." He even joked about the climate of the fight and the fact that his life was supposedly in danger. Liston is "gonna be scared by this," Ali said. "It might be smoky in that arena, and you couldn't see good. I'm gonna say, 'Sonny, I'm fast and you're slow. You might catch one of them bullets. Let me knock you out so we can both get out of here.'"

In addition to being his normal quick-witted self, Ali looked sharp physically. Reports of Liston were not so glowing. *The New York Times* wrote that Liston looked "sluggish and flat-footed" during his training.

> "If he'd stop all of that hollering, he wouldn't have a hernia."
>
> —SONNY LISTON, after Ali's emergency hernia surgery

Sitting poolside at a Holiday Inn the day before the fight, Ali played coy when asked for a prediction for the fight. "I can only say this," he said. "Come early. There will be a lot of excitement for those who dare to dare. Just wait and see. I may not throw a single punch in the first round. Then again, I may go right out and get him." Ali pointed toward the ground: "That's where he's going down. That man Liston is scared."

Ali got serious when the Lewiston venue was mentioned, calling it a "disgrace." "This is the biggest fight of all time, and it's gonna be held in a little country arena," Ali said. "Why, I drew 17,000 fans just to see me fight in the Golden Gloves."

By fight time, an estimated 80 million radio listeners tuned in, and more than 250 theaters and arenas in the United States and Canada showed the closed-circuit television broadcast. In addition, the fight also was the

first to be shown live overseas, via satellite. The fruits of the electronic age would bring in approximately $5 million.

Spectators were still being seated when the first round began. They wound up missing the entire fight. Within the first minute, Ali landed a right cross followed by a right to Liston's temple. He then landed another right to the side of Liston's head, sending him to the canvas.

With Liston on the deck, Ali stood over his victim, yelling: "Get up and fight!" The photographs of this moment would become the most famous in boxing history. Meanwhile former heavyweight champion Jersey Joe Walcott, who served as the fight's referee, urged Ali to go to a neutral corner so he could start his count.

Ali explained that he did not immediately report to a neutral corner because Liston had fallen "a half-minute quicker than I thought he would" and that he wanted him to get up and fight some more. "I tried to tell

"Get up and fight!"

—ALI to Liston after Sonny collapsed to the canvas in the first round

him to get up, but I guess he was hurt," Ali said.

Here is where the fight got confusing: Liston got up and actually began to fight again before Walcott counted him out. But somewhere in this process, long-time ring expert Nat Fleischer called to Walcott, telling him that Liston had been down 12 seconds. Fleischer was not an official, merely someone watching the fight, but Walcott—upon being notified about how much time had passed—signaled that the fight was over and that Ali had successfully defended his crown.

"I did not count out Liston," Walcott said. "I was told that he was on the floor 12 seconds. Then I awarded the knockout."

The fight was over within two and a half minutes. Many of the sparse crowd of 4,280 booed the finish while others shouted "fake" as Ali stood in the ring offering commentary on the fight. "Look at me float like a butterfly," he said in the ring while watching footage. "He can't hit me. Look, I'm too fast."

Opposite: Ali shouts in celebration while standing over a knocked-out Liston in Round 1 of their 1965 rematch`in Lewiston, Maine. "Get up and fight," the champ yelled. Ali had predicted an early finish to his title defense. He had pointed to the ground in the days leading up to the bout and told reporters, "That's where he's going down."

There was some confusion after Liston (*rear*) returned to his feet after going down in the first round of his 1965 rematch with Ali. After officials ruled that the former champ had indeed been on the canvas long enough for a knockout, Ali was hoisted off his feet in celebration of his impressive heavyweight title defense.

Once again the victor against Liston despite being the underdog, Ali chastised those who had doubted him. He ranted about how all the critics had favored Liston because he was a former convict and that he was dismissed because of his righteous lifestyle.

Ali called the phantom punch "the anchor punch." He credited former comic and movie actor Stepin Fetchit, who was part of his entourage, for teaching him the punch that, according to Ali, former heavyweight champion Jack Johnson "took to his grave." Ali said he had studied the punch, which was an overhand right that was "so fast it even scares me."

"It's a twisting right-handed snap, and you twist your hand as you hit," he said. "I had to time my rhythm and balance and hit him just when he was coming at me. If you got

hit with it, all of you [reporters in the locker room] would be out."

Ali's berating of Liston ended after the fight. "I'm not going to down Sonny Liston," Ali said. "I feel sorry for him. You fellows don't care about him now that he's lost."

Liston explained his loss simply by stating, "I over-trained for that fight." But many believed that the fix had been in. Years after the bout, Ali remembered how people had talked about his first fight with Liston being fixed, so he wanted to "whup him bad" the second time around, adding: "I didn't want him making excuses or quitting. I wanted him to get up so I could show everybody how great I was."

In the end, Muhammad Ali had defended his title, but Liston took to his grave the answer to whether he had taken a dive in either of their fights.

PATTERSON'S HUMILIATION

Ali had altered his prediction for defeating Patterson in 1965, first calling for an early knockout but later promising to punish the former champion. By ducking Patterson's blows, landing plenty of his own, and taunting his opponent relentlessly, Ali did exactly that over 12 rounds before winning by TKO.

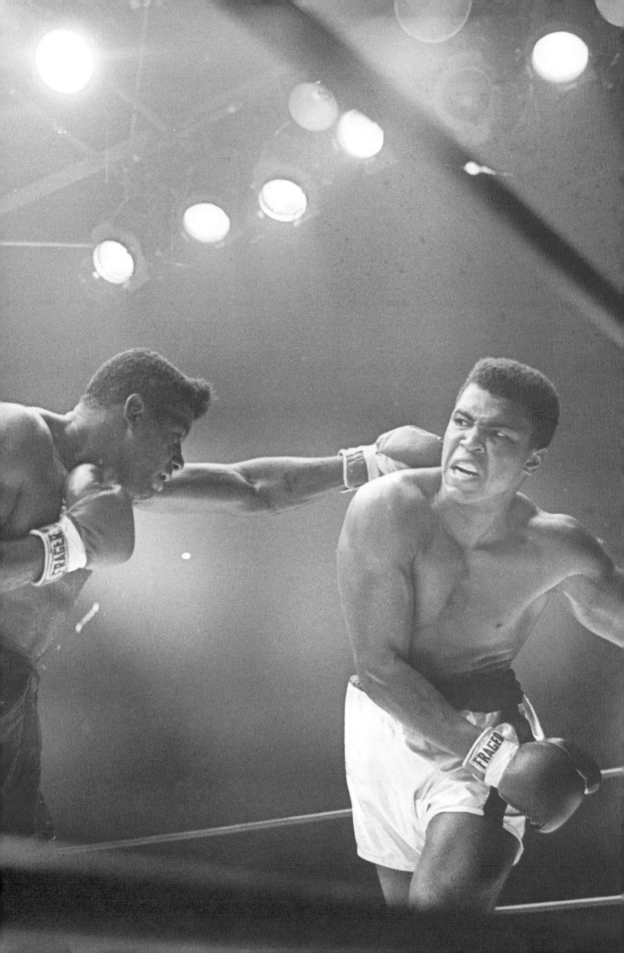

PATTERSON'S HUMILIATION

Never shy with his opponents or his fans, Ali had the ladies smiling as he signed autographs in Boston in November 1965. He would not be so kind days later in his title defense against Floyd Patterson.

Though sent to a reform school during his troubled youth, Floyd Patterson grew up to be a soft-spoken and reflective man. Legendary sportswriter W. C. Heinz called him "a shy, sensitive soul-searcher." When Patterson did speak, Heinz wrote, "it is with a purity reminiscent of Joe Louis."

In 1956 a 21-year-old Patterson knocked out Archie Moore to become the youngest heavyweight champion in boxing history. He lost the crown to Ingemar Johansson in 1959, but he won it back in a rematch the following year. It was an achievement he called the most gratifying moment of his life—a life conducted largely out of the limelight.

Patterson's disposition worked in stark contrast to that of the man who, in the mid-1960s, adopted the Muslim name Muhammad Ali. While Patterson's stay at boxing's summit was quiet and unassuming, Ali's arrival a few years later was nothing of the sort.

Ali became a top contender as the brash, young Cassius Clay. He joined the Black Muslim separatist movement as Cassius X before wresting the title from Sonny Liston in 1964. He then insisted on being called Muhammad Ali in the weeks leading up to his bout with Patterson on November 22, 1965.

During a break from his actual fight training, Ali prepared for his verbal barrages. Here, he practices his "Float like a butterfly, sting like a bee" mantra with his cornerman, Bundini Brown, during a 1965 press conference at his training camp in Chicopee, Massachusetts. Ali was prepping for his fight with Patterson.

Ali was relentless in his verbal attacks toward former heavyweight champion and former sparring partner Floyd Patterson. Ali, who showed up at Patterson's training camp on January 21, 1965, called Patterson "The Rabbit" and challenged him to a fight right there in the training ring. Patterson tried to keep his poise but at one point replied, "Let's do it." Ali left without punches being traded.

Patterson, a Roman Catholic, refused to do so. His convictions ran so deep that he stepped out of the shadows and into the spotlight when addressing the subjects of Ali and the Black Muslims, thus beginning a rivalry with the fast-talking heavyweight champion. It was a rivalry that would keep the media enthralled with the prospect of a bout that—were it to happen—likely would not last more than a handful of rounds. Patterson, at age 30, was seemingly past his prime, and Ali had defeated the "unbeatable" Sonny Liston.

Long before their date was on the calendar, on a spring night in 1964, Patterson was watching television in bed when Ali appeared on his screen calling him a sissy. "If I'm such a sissy, Clay," Patterson reportedly yelled at the TV, "why don't you fight me? I'll fight you for nothing. I'll pay for your sparring partners. I'd gladly lose money on the fight."

Over the next several months, there was considerable interest in seeing such a bout. Patterson's people offered Ali a $750,000 guarantee, saying their fighter would box for no purse in an effort to take the title from "Cassius X and the Black Muslims." It was not enough money, Ali's handlers insisted, for a fight of that magnitude.

Ali proposed a winner-take-all match, saying he would give his earnings to the Black Muslims and suggesting that Patterson—in the unlikely event of an upset—could fill the Catholic Church's coffers with his winnings. "I'll play with him for 10 rounds," Ali told a Chicago television station. "He has been talking about my religion. I'll just paw him. Then after I beat him, I'll convert him."

That, too, failed to produce a date. Ali and Patterson went their separate ways, but not without delivering verbal jabs when opportunities surfaced. "Cassius X is part of a hate group in this country," Patterson said in 1964. "He's not a good example for Negroes. I'd like to fight him so much and feel determined because I'd like to get the championship away from the Black Muslims."

Ali continually called Patterson "the Rabbit," claiming that the challenger was skittish and scared. He strolled into Patterson's camp in January 1965, while Patterson trained for a February date with George Chuvalo, hurling insults and demanding that Patterson call him by his Muslim name.

"The name you were born with is Cassius Clay," Patterson said.

"Cassius Clay is a slave name," Ali shouted, waving his fist as flashbulbs popped and reporters scrawled each word. "I'm free.... You got a slave name.... You ain't nothin' but an Uncle Tom Negro.... You Uncle Tom, I'll jump right in there on you now."

Patterson had lost twice in the first round to Liston, the man Ali knocked out in 1964

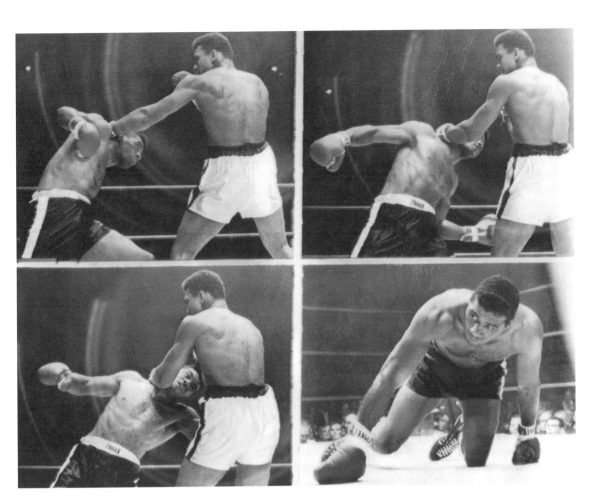

for the title. It was a fact Ali would not let Patterson forget. "It wouldn't be fair," Ali said of Patterson, "for a man of his abilities—such a puny, light man who can't take a punch—to stand up for all the Catholics in the world."

Patterson's unanimous decision over Chuvalo in February 1965 and Ali's first-round stopping of Liston in their rematch three months later finally allowed this war of words to become a rumble in the ring. Patterson would get a shot at the heavyweight title, and a chance to put his convictions to the ultimate test, on November 22 at the Convention Center in Las Vegas.

Ali, who would earn close to $750,000—double Patterson's take—was made a 7-to-1 favorite by the betting public, although Patterson seemed to be the sentimental choice among fans. Ali had previously predicted an early knockout when the prospect of fighting Patterson was broached. As the fight neared, however, the champ seemed to be leaning in a different direction. Less than three weeks before the bout, Ali said he would "punish" Patterson and give him "a good beating so he won't have any excuses."

This sixth-round barrage by Ali could have—some say should have—ended his 1965 heavyweight title match against Patterson. However, after knocking his opponent down with a series of well-timed punches, Ali was content to dance and jab against the former champion, dominating a fight that was eventually stopped in the 12th round.

"He has been talking about my religion. . . . After I beat him, I'll convert him."

—ALI, on Floyd Patterson

Ali promised a surprise at the weigh-in, and he was true to his word. Shockingly, the champ was stoic. He did not address Patterson, and at one point he waved the challenger onto the scale first. Ali later posed with him, side-by-side, without uttering a word.

Security was doubled for the fight. No one said why, but Ali's contingent of Black Muslim supporters from all corners of the country certainly played a part. Nine months earlier, a Black Muslim had assassinated Malcolm X. "We don't want to take any chances," one sheriff's lieutenant said.

Once the bell sounded, the silent treatment that Ali had given Patterson at the weigh-in was over. The champ had plenty to say, with both his words and actions. The most dominant boxer in the world likely could have named his round for a knockout. At 210, he was 16 pounds heavier than Patterson. He also owned an eight-inch reach advantage, a three-inch edge in height, and, at 23, was seven years younger. His superiority was obvious.

Instead of using his considerable gifts to put an early end to the evening, Ali did not throw a serious punch in the first round. Instead, he danced and showboated and taunted, yelling "No contest!" and "Get me a contender!" When Ali finally began throwing jabs in the second round, he did so while jeering "Boop! Boop! Boop!"

Patterson was helpless against his quicker, stronger, and better-conditioned foe. In the fourth round, the challenger's back gave out, causing him to crouch for most of the duration. A healthier posture would not have mattered. *The New York Times* explained, "It seemed as if all Clay wanted to do tonight, before 7,402 paying spectators including several movie stars, was to destroy Patterson forever as a boxer and as a dignified human being."

The champ's verbal barrage was so relentless that referee Harry Krause told him to "shut up" during the fourth round. In the fifth and sixth rounds, Ali landed hard jabs over and over, snapping Patterson's head back. The former champ slumped to one knee in the sixth, drawing a mandatory eight count, but the count began several seconds late because Ali took his time moving to a neutral corner.

Ali denied having "carried" Patterson for 12 rounds, crediting his challenger for fighting gamely and noting that he had injured his right hand in the eighth round. However, that sixth-round scene was telling. Ali could have finished off Patterson then—if not much sooner—but sent only gentle jabs toward his opponent once the eight count had been administered. Ali resumed his dancing in subsequent rounds, forcing Patterson to lunge wildly after him with hooks that met only air.

Ali danced, taunted, shook his head, landed jabs at will, and even waved at Patterson from his stool between rounds. Those in Patterson's corner tried their best to block their fighter's view. Once the bell sounded, however, there was little they—or anyone—could do for Patterson.

By the 12th round, Krause had seen enough. With Patterson's knees buckling, the champ thoroughly enjoying himself, and fans shouting for Ali—or "Clay," among the white patrons—to throw a knockout punch, the referee stopped the fight. A brief scuffle ensued between police and a member of the Black Muslims who had charged the ring at the end of the bout, but order was quickly restored.

Two of the three men scoring the fight had Ali ahead by 10 points on their cards; the other had a nine-point cushion. Ali's 22nd professional victory without a loss was indeed a one-sided affair, but it was one that should have ended much sooner.

Immediately after the fight, and at the news conference the following day, Ali heaped praise on Patterson. He told reporters that Patterson could fight successfully for another five years, because he would never have to face a boxer with his speed and power again. He praised Floyd for fighting like a man. He called Patterson an honorable man, and he praised him as humble for not making an excuse of his back injury.

For his part, Patterson thanked Ali for "not making it difficult." He called the champ Muhammad Ali, rather than Cassius Clay or Cassius X. If hard feelings existed between the two, they did not surface after the fight like they did before or during.

This, of course, was theater. Ali did indeed stretch Patterson to 12 rounds for a reason. Two months later, the champ admitted as much while still speaking of his opponent in reverent terms. "Every fighter should take it easy on a man if he is seriously hurt," Ali said in a taped television segment for ABC's *Wide World of Sports* in January 1966. "I'd rather hear you talk about me carrying a man than killing him."

History recalls the Ali-Patterson fight not so much as an exercise in preserving the life and health of an overmatched fighter, but an exercise in humiliation. Patterson's prefight words toward Ali were out of character, and Ali made him eat every one.

Ali, of course, went on to further his legacy as "The Greatest," while Patterson's best days were behind him. Floyd did give champion Jimmy Ellis all he could handle in a 1968 WBA title bout in Sweden, after Ali had been stripped of his title. Patterson lost a controversial decision in his effort to become the first three-time champ.

The humble Patterson also proved that Ali's "Uncle Tom" remarks were off base. Legendary sportscaster Howard Cosell, in his autobiography, recounted how Patterson and baseball pioneer Jackie Robinson were once in the Deep South during the civil rights movement and came upon "white only" and "colored only" water fountains. Patterson, Cosell wrote, drank from both fountains in front of a crowd that included several whites, then turned and exclaimed, "Tastes like the same water."

Had he been there, Ali might have cheered his one-time nemesis.

Referee Harry Krause gestures over a fallen Patterson in the sixth round of a 1965 heavyweight title bout in Las Vegas. Ali dominated the former champ, but he put his hardest punches away for a while after the sixth-round knockdown, stretching his pummeling of Patterson to 12 rounds.

STILL PERFECT

Fans in England embraced Ali, even if the best fighters in their homeland might have been better off without the American's overseas visits. In his second consecutive title defense in Great Britain, Ali sent Brian London to the canvas in the third round, thanks to crushing right hands like this one, on August 6, 1966.

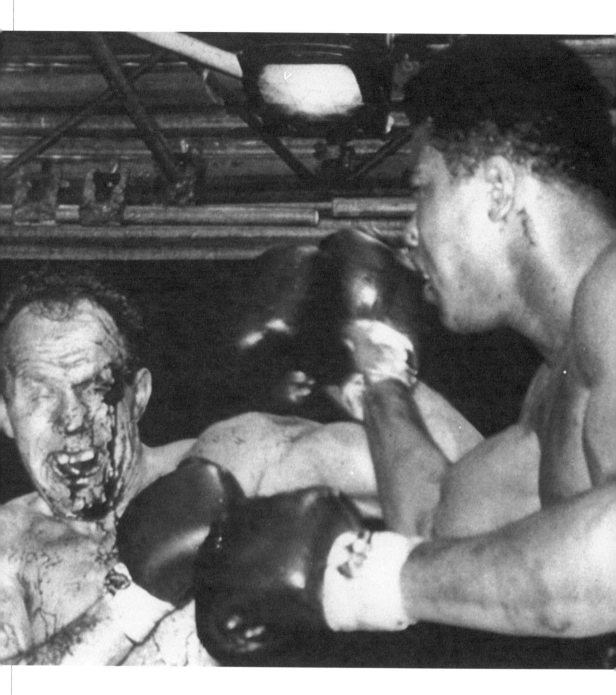

The first heavyweight championship fight in England in nearly
60 years turned into a bloody mess for hometown favorite
Henry Cooper on May 21, 1966. Ali zeroed in on the cut above
Cooper's left eye in the sixth round moments before the gash
caused the referee to stop the bout.

STILL PERFECT

Ali was a master in the ring but went virtually ignored in the canine world, at least when it came to this corgi. If Ali and sparring partner Jimmy Ellis couldn't get the pooch to fetch a ball, at least they had the luxury of knowing that, one week later, British heavyweight champ Henry Cooper would have no choice but to pay attention to Ali during their 1966 rematch in London.

It is hard enough being the heavyweight champion of the world. Attempting to fight the United States government at the same time seems like a ludicrous proposition. Ali made it look easy. He dominated the sport of boxing, a daunting task for any great athlete, and he never backed away from his social and religious beliefs.

Ali was scheduled to open the 1966 campaign by defending his heavyweight title against Ernie Terrell. At this juncture of his career, Ali was no stranger to adversity, but the biggest controversy of his career was simmering. In February, Ali's draft status was changed from exempt to 1A. He felt that the sudden turnaround was punishment because he had aligned himself with the Nation of Islam. When news broke of his draft status, Ali made comments to reporters that many people considered unpatriotic. Among them was the now famous line "I ain't got no quarrel with the Vietcong."

The public outcry over that statement put the Terrell fight in immediate jeopardy. Suddenly, the fight lost its sanction, locale, and many of its sponsors. In an attempt to salvage the date, promoters suggested taking the fight to Canada. When Terrell

George Chuvalo covers up as Ali launches a flurry of punches to his head in the 15th round of their Toronto fight on March 29, 1966. Chuvalo fought dirty, hitting Ali below the belt, but Muhammad won a unanimous decision.

> "George's head is the hardest thing I've ever punched."
>
> —ALI, on George Chuvalo

was offered less money and no guarantee on the purse, he turned the offer down. There was, however, someone still willing to fight Ali, even if it was on 17 days notice: Toronto's George Chuvalo, an aggressive, durable heavyweight who had lost a decision to Terrell four months earlier.

The date was finally settled, even if Ali's boxing future was not. Muhammad would meet Chuvalo on March 29, 1966, at Maple Leaf Gardens in Toronto. Ali was favored 7-1 to retain the title. Going into the contest, Chuvalo said, "I can knock him out if I fight my best." Ali, meanwhile, predicted he would become the first man to knock Chuvalo out.

When the opening bell rang, Ali was finally at peace. Inside the ring, he was free to express himself as an artist, and few who ever laced on gloves did it better than him during this fight. He was graceful, aggressive, and focused. Early in the bout, he waved the Canadian on, yelling, "Harder, harder!"

Ali's jab dictated the pace, and his movement made him nearly impossible to catch. He danced—in and out, side to side—while popping his stiff left jab. Chuvalo's face began to swell in Round 3, and Ali increased the punishment in Round 5—distorting Chuvalo's cheeky visage with each blistering combination. He bounced nimbly to the left and to the right while Chuvalo followed like an obedient puppy on a leash. To his credit, the granite-chinned Chuvalo absorbed every punch. He waded forward, lunging after the champion, hoping to land the one punch that could turn it all around.

In the buildup to the fight, Chuvalo had promised to turn this exhibition of the "manly art" into a street fight. He lived up to his word, repeatedly hitting Ali below the belt line. None of it mattered. Ali swept the scorecards for a 73-65, 74-63, and 74-62 unanimous decision before 13,540 fans.

"George's head is the hardest thing I've ever punched," said Ali after the fight. "I hit him with seven or eight good punches. But I had to back off because he's so strong and you just wear yourself out against a guy like that."

Chuvalo, meanwhile, was impressed by the champion. "Ali had the size, the speed, the natural smarts, great ability to take a punch," he said. "He didn't have a real big punch, but he didn't have to. He had everything else.… He thought he was God in the ring. Everything was working for him. Everything he did was right."

The draft controversy continued to make Ali a hard sell in the United States. He

Though neither gained fame for his musical abilities, that did not stop NBC *Tonight Show* host Johnny Carson and heavyweight champion Ali from putting on a show in 1967 for a photographer in New York. Carson and Ali did share a love for quips and one-liners.

maintained that, as a minister of Islam, he would not go to war based on religious grounds. If drafted, he would refuse induction. Unwelcome in the U.S., Ali took his title and his show to Europe.

The champ's first fight would be against former nemesis Henry Cooper, whom he had fought in 1963. And while Ali had only gotten better since their first meeting, Cooper's career was in decline. Still, there was that matter of the knockdown in their first bout, courtesy of Henry's left hook, and that was enough to pique the curiosity of the British boxing faithful.

The rematch took place on May 21, 1966, before 46,000 fans at Arsenal Stadium in London. It was the first time England had hosted a heavyweight title fight since 1908. The result was all too familiar, as Ali opened a terrible cut above Cooper's left eye and scored a technical knockout in the sixth round. The Queen and her subjects would not wait nearly as long for the next heavyweight title fight. Ten weeks later, on August 6, Ali returned to fight Brian London at Earls Court. Ali was a 10-1 favorite and quickly showed why, knocking out London with a flurry of punches capped by a right cross to the jaw in the third round.

"I'm sorry," London told reporters after the fight. "You told me he was good, but nobody said he was that good. There were so many punches, I didn't know where they were coming from."

The European boxing fans accepted Ali as a sportsman, cheering him wherever he went. The draft controversy was part of his life, but the fallout hardly stretched across the Atlantic. Overseas, the fans were accommodating and the competition was not very strenuous. Thus, Ali returned and defended his title against Karl Mildenberger in Frankfurt, Germany, on September 10, 1966.

Mildenberger was the reigning European champion and had not lost a fight in more than four years. He was also a southpaw. It hardly mattered once the bell rang.

At this point of Ali's career, he was as close to unbeatable as any fighter had ever been. His speed was intoxicating and his movements flawless. He was also beginning to sit down on his punches—planting his feet long enough to get the full weight of his body behind his shots. It was a painful reality for Mildenberger. He was cut above both eyes in Round 4 and dropped by a right hand in Round 5. Mildenberger was seemingly defenseless.

Yet Ali inexplicably slowed the pace, allowing the fight to continue and the German to recover. Ali casually dropped Mildenberger twice more before winning by knockout in Round 12.

Europe may have provided a respite from bad publicity and public outrage, but it was time for Ali to return home. Few had forgotten the draft controversy, and even fewer had forgiven Ali. Even though his last four fights had been in foreign countries, he was about to fight before a hostile audience.

"It weighed on Muhammad," said Jimmy Ellis, Ali's sparring partner at the time who would later win a share of the heavyweight title when the champion was in exile. "You would never know it watching him fight or watching him train. He was in his prime during that time period. But the draft and how people knocked him over…it was on his mind a lot. He just never showed it to the world. All you saw was "Float like a butterfly, sting like a bee.'"

Ali floated and stung like never before on November 14, 1966, at the Houston Astrodome. He defended his title against veteran contender Cleveland Williams. Throughout his European swing, Ali had toyed with his opponents. Williams was 33 years old, and he had recently overcome a gunshot wound to the abdomen. But he was still a dangerous puncher and a durable commodity in the heavyweight division.

The media remained critical of Ali, but the Louisville Lip's confidence never waned. He told his opponent in the prefight buildup, "I don't get hit," and it appeared to be true. When it came time to fight, Williams struggled to reach his elusive opponent. The veteran may have had a statuesque physique, but Ali made him look like a statue. He was that slow, at least compared to the champ.

"You're acting just like another Uncle Tom, Floyd Patterson, and I'm going to give you a good punishment, too." —ALI, to Ernie Terrell

Boxing historians often point to this fight as Ali's finest. His left jab was piercing, softening Williams the way a fastball breaks in a catcher's mitt. In Round 2, Ali put power punches behind the jab and dropped Williams three times. Cleveland appeared out after the third knockdown, but he was saved by the bell. It was almost impossible for Williams to mount an attack because he was perpetually defending against Ali's blows. They were swift, they were sharp, and they landed often.

For a brief moment in Round 3, the champion introduced the "Ali Shuffle," sliding his feet front to back and back to front, before unloading a barrage of punches that dropped Williams for the fourth and final time. On the air, announcer Howard Cosell said Ali was "the most devastating fighter who ever lived."

Chuvalo was sitting ringside for the bout. "Everything came together in Houston when he fought Cleveland Williams," Chuvalo said. "Ali was at his absolute best right before the exile."

The Ali legacy was about to grow, but perhaps not in a way he hoped. Twelve weeks after the Williams fight, Ali returned to the Astrodome to finally meet Terrell. On paper, the matchup was a good one. Terrell, now holder of the WBA heavyweight title, was unbeaten over the last five years and was considered Ali's toughest test since Liston. He was 6'6" and had a three-inch reach advantage over Ali, a potential hazard for a fighter who likes to box from a distance.

Ali was a champion presiding over a divided nation. He was either loved or loathed. And those who yearned to see Ali defeated found a new reason to root against him. At a press conference for the fight at the offices of Madison Square Garden, Ali

While Ali would not have fared well against Wilt Chamberlain on the hardwood, it's also a safe bet that Wilt's reach of 90-plus inches would not have saved him from a pummeling by Ali in the ring. The two, shown here in 1967, discussed a boxing match, but level heads prevailed.

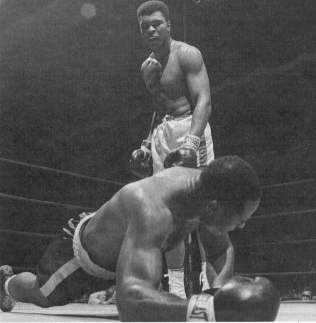

Zora Folley was no match for Ali on March 22, 1967, at Madison Square Garden. In his ninth consecutive successful defense of his heavyweight belt, Ali delivered a knockout punch in the seventh round, looking down at his opponent as Folley hit the canvas.

launched into a hate-filled diatribe because Terrell referred to him as Cassius Clay.

"Why do you call me Clay?" Ali asked. "You know my right name is Muhammad Ali."

"I met you as Cassius Clay," Terrell responded.

"It takes an Uncle Tom Negro to keep calling me by my slave name.… You are an Uncle Tom," Ali said.

Ali then removed his suit jacket and lunged toward Terrell, swinging with open-handed blows. The diatribe resumed. "You're acting just like another Uncle Tom, Floyd Patterson, and I'm going to give you a good punishment, too," Ali said. "I'm going to make you an example to the world."

Whatever hope Terrell had for an upset dissolved in a flurry of punches. Ali's ring superiority was evident immediately. Terrell's best weapon was his long, left jab. Ali nullified it with his own jab. By Round 4, Terrell's left eye was nearly swollen shut. By Round 5, he was cut above the right eye. But instead of finishing off his wounded opponent, Ali prolonged the fight, taunting Terrell round after round.

"What's my name?" Ali shouted throughout the fight. He would land a barrage of punches, pause, and shout the question again. Terrell never answered; he simply waded forward and accepted the punishment. When it was over, his left cheekbone was fractured and Ali copped a unanimous decision.

The press that followed was brutal. Arthur Daley of *The New York Times* called Ali "malicious and mean" and added, "The more he improves as a fighter, the more apparent becomes his retrogression as a man."

One thing was certain: Ali kept improving. On March 22, 1967, he knocked out contender Zora Folley in the seventh round. It was the ninth successful defense of his heavyweight title. He was 25 years old and had a record of 29-0. It was clear that Ali was not going to lose his title inside the ring. The forces that were looming outside of the ropes, however, were another story.

HELL NO,
ALI WON'T GO

Ali, sitting in his Chicago home in 1968, reads a book written by Black Muslim leader Elijah Muhammad. Ali, having been stripped of his heavyweight title because of his objection to joining the war in Vietnam, had become a Black Muslim minister, following Muhammad in a life of study and preaching.

HELL NO, ALI WON'T GO

Ali is greeted as he stops on the step of the Veterans Administration office in his hometown of Louisville on March 17, 1966. Ali, with the help of attorney Edward Jocko *(behind him, in dark coat and hat),* was appealing his 1-A draft classification. He had no intention of joining the war effort in Vietnam.

Ali's journey into the defining period of his life began shortly after his first fight with Sonny Liston in 1964, when he announced his conversion to the Nation of Islam and stated that he had assumed the name of "Cassius X.""X" stood for the unknown last name that slave owners had stripped away from his family. Soon he changed his name to Muhammad Ali.

Though certainly intelligent, Ali was not a well-educated man. In fact, he received a military deferment in 1964 when he failed to qualify due to tests that showed that his spelling and writing skills were below average. A revision of the tests in early 1966 prompted the military to reclassify Ali as 1-A, which triggered the series of events that led to his being banned from boxing and being stripped of his heavyweight title.

Upon being reclassified, Ali noted in February 1966 that he had "no quarrel with them Vietcong." Ali's position on the war in Vietnam surprised many and cast him as a traitor to others. And like many of Ali's actions throughout his life, this one was unique. Politicians, the media, even college students had yet to hop on the antiwar bandwagon.

Ali had become a Black Muslim minister, and as such became a conscientious objector to serving in the military—a stance

In March 1967, one month before his scheduled induction into the U.S. Army, Ali stood with human rights leader Dr. Martin Luther King, Jr., in a Louisville court in an effort to block his call to duty. The court refused. "I'm fighting for the freedom of my people," Ali told reporters.

perceived by some as odd given the fact that he made his living as a fighter.

"In a boxing ring, we have a referee to stop the fight if it gets too brutal," Ali said. "The intention is not to kill, as it is in war. We don't use machinery, artillery, guns. You can't compare boxing with a war; it's different."

In March 1967, J. Allen Sherman, the chairman of Local Draft Board 47 in Louisville, Kentucky, announced Ali's induction date as April 11, 1967. If Ali chose to disregard his induction, he faced penalties for selective service evasion that called for five years of imprisonment and a $10,000 fine.

"My decision is made," Ali told reporters. "But I have to answer to the government, not no reporters. If necessary, I'll have to die for what I believe in. I'm fighting for the freedom of my people."

Ali's lawyers managed to delay his induction date based on the contention that Ali's residence was in Houston, not Louisville. But he gained little from the move, as his induction date was pushed back just 17 days, to April 28.

At 8 A.M. on April 28, Ali reported to the United States Custom House on San Jacinto Street in downtown Houston and went to the third floor, home of the Armed Forces Examining and Entrance Station. Ali

> "In a boxing ring, we have a referee to stop the fight if it gets too brutal. The intention is not to kill, as it is in war."
>
> —ALI

then refused to take the ceremonious and necessary physical step forward in order to take the oath.

Afterward, Lieutenant Colonel J. Edwin McKee, commander of the station, informed reporters about Ali's action, or lack thereof. Because Ali refused to take the oath, his case was sent to the U.S. attorney general's office and the national and local selective service boards. Ali maintained that his vocation was as a Black Muslim minister and that boxing was his avocation. He read from a statement afterward.

"It is the light of my consciousness as a Muslim minister and my own personal convictions that I take my stand in rejecting the call to be inducted in the armed services," he stated. "I do so with the full realization of its implications and possible consequences. I have searched my conscience and I find I cannot be true to my belief in my religion by accepting such a call."

Ali called his decision "private and individual" and noted that he understood the magnitude of making the decision.

"In taking it, I am dependent solely upon Allah as the final judge of these actions brought about by my own conscience," he said. "I strongly object to the fact that so many newspapers have given the American

Opposite: Ali and his supporters were all smiles in Houston after Ali refused to step forward and take his Armed Forces induction oath on April 28, 1967. While hundreds of fans gathered in the streets to cheer the former boxing champ, the authorities did not share their support. Ali was convicted of draft evasion and sentenced to five years in prison, but he was released pending appeals.

A seated Elijah Muhammad, the Black Muslim leader and one of Ali's most influential mentors, approves as Ali addresses a crowd at the Black Muslim Annual Convention in Chicago on February 25, 1968.

public and the world the impression that I have only two alternatives in taking this stand: either I go to jail or go to the Army. There is another alternative and that alternative is justice. If justice prevails, if my constitutional rights are upheld, I will be forced to go neither to the Army nor jail. In the end, I am confident that justice will come my way, for the truth must eventually prevail….

"I am looking forward to immediately continuing my profession. As to the threat voiced by certain elements to 'strip' me of my title, this is merely a continuation of the same artificially induced prejudice and discrimination. Regardless of the difference in my outlook, I insist upon my right to pursue my livelihood in accordance with the same rights granted to other men and women who have disagreed with the policies of whatever administration was in power at the time."

Ali also addressed his future as heavyweight champion—and the possibility of a round-robin tournament to determine a champion once he was stripped of the title. He maintained that he held the title not because it was given to him but because he earned it.

"Those who want to take it and hold a series of auction-type bouts not only do me a disservice, but actually disgrace themselves," Ali said. "I am certain that fairminded people through America would never accept such a title-holder."

Ali's title was stripped. He was convicted of draft evasion and sentenced to five years in prison, but he was released on bail while numerous appeals ran their course.

While in exile, Ali received offers to fight abroad, but he could not engage them since his passport was taken away from him. He was not allowed to leave the United States, nor was he able to earn a living in the ring in his native country.

Ali wasn't allowed to fight, but he could see the future. He understood the pulse of a country in strife and the direction sentiments were drifting. And being realistic, he thought he would serve his five-year prison sentence.

"If you think I'm a big man now, because I'm a fighter, wait until five years from now when I come out," Ali said. "I'll be bigger yet. This thing is much bigger than boxing."

With Ali out of the picture, the heavyweight title belonged to no one. Plenty of suitors were interested, though.

In the aftermath of the New York State Athletic Commission revoking Ali's boxing license, the World Boxing Association took away his crown and came up with the idea of holding an eight-man elimination tournament to determine a new heavyweight champion. Chosen to participate in the tournament were Oscar Bonavena, Floyd Patterson, Ernie Terrell, Thad Spencer, Jimmy Ellis, Jerry Quarry, Joe Frazier, and Karl Mildenberger.

Frazier made a sound decision by electing not to participate in the tournament. He had an undefeated record and already held the distinction as the WBA's No. 1 contender. In Frazier's mind, the tournament would play out and he would have the first crack at the winner, so why risk an upset by participating in the tournament? Leotis Martin took Frazier's place.

Meanwhile, Ali dismissed the tournament. "All right, if you want to talk boxing, I'll talk boxing," Ali told a *Chicago Tribune* reporter. "You take this tournament they have to find a new champion. It's silly; want to know why? Have you ever seen my heavyweight championship belt?"

Ali showed the belt to a reporter and it read: "To Cassius Clay of Louisville, Kentucky." The belt designated Clay the champion after knocking out Liston.

"When those great old-time champions fought—Louis or Tunney or Sullivan or Corbett—there was never a time when a man could sit in the audience and say 'I can lick the champ' without everyone thinking he's crazy," Ali said. "But I'm going to be sitting ringside when they hold this championship fight, and I'm going to say, 'I can lick either one of 'em,' and everyone sitting around me will know I can, too."

Spencer began the tournament by defeating Terrell. Ellis defeated Martin, Quarry beat Patterson, and Bonavena outlasted Mildenberger. Ellis then defeated Bonavena and Quarry beat Spencer to set up a title bout between Ellis and Quarry, which Ellis won in 15 rounds. Meanwhile, Frazier squared off against Buster Mathis and knocked him out in 11 rounds. That set up the prospect of a title match between Ellis and Frazier.

But a fight between the two did not immediately take place, fueling speculation about who would be the champion, Ellis or Frazier? Or would Ali return to the ring to claim his title?

Frazier continued to box in the interim, defeating Manuel Ramos before squaring off against Bonavena with a highly visible spectator in the stands. In the later rounds of the fight—won by Frazier—that spectator, Ali, stood and yelled at Frazier.

"You're a disgrace to the colored race," Ali said. "Frazier, you fight like a woman. Why, you're hanging all over that man."

Ali critiqued the match by calling the fight a "slugging match" and "not boxing." "I could take both of them," Ali said. "They're both made to order for me. See that Bonavena jab? I could get off 12 of them—brrr-brrr-brrr—just like that."

After Bonavena, Frazier defeated Dave Zyglewcz and Quarry. Meanwhile, Ellis' matches with Henry Cooper and Greg Peralta were canceled before he defended his title against Patterson, which Ellis won unimpressively by decision. Frazier and Ellis finally were scheduled to fight in February 1970.

Just prior to the fight, Ali said he would give his belt to the winner of the fight since he had decided to retire. Frazier defeated Ellis with a fifth-round knockout to claim the WBA heavyweight title.

The boxing world continued to turn without Ali, whose persona grew daily while legions of U.S. citizens gravitated toward antiwar stances. Ali's stance now looked far more fashionable.

"I was branded a traitor for saying we had no business being at war in Vietnam," he said, "but six months later we had

With Ali having been stripped of his heavyweight title, Jimmy Ellis (*left*) and Joe Frazier each had a claim to the crown in December 1969 as they held up copies of a pact for their impending bout in New York. Frazier knocked out Ellis in the fifth round at Madison Square Garden in February 1970 to unify the heavyweight championship in Ali's absence.

three fellows—[Robert] Kennedy, [Eugene] McCarthy, and [George] McGovern—saying the same thing as they tried to win the presidential nomination."

Even in this changing climate, Ali in mid-1970 believed the government wanted to make an example of him. He still believed that jail was in his future.

"I'd like to fight Joe Frazier for the heavyweight title, but he'll probably have to wait until I'm out of jail," Ali said. "I honestly said I didn't want any part of no war in Vietnam. There is no reason for us to be over there taking human lives. I was alone when I defied the government the first time. Since then there are thousands who have been more defiant. I've seen 'em burn draft cards, insult the flag, and run to Canada—then turn into vandals when they see a statue of the president of the United States.

"I still carry my draft card. I haven't insulted the flag or run to Canada. I've preached no violence; I've preached peace. Yet these hippies have laughed and said they'll get less time, and less punishment, for all the trouble they've caused than I'll get for acting according to my religious beliefs and the beliefs of my people. So obviously, I'm an example.

"I don't think we should be killing people. We should be feeding hungry people and curing sick people. I've always said that. At one time, my attitude toward the war was very unpopular. Now lots of people have changed. Time always brings change.

"Long ago I could have gotten off the hook by going into the induction center and saying I was sorry. That would have been a popular action. In these days, I was one of the few who dared defy popular opinion. Today I'd be unpopular with millions of Americans if I reversed my stand. The pressure is so great today that it'd be almost impossible, even if I wanted, to say that I'm sorry."

In September 1970, a federal court order found that the New York State Athletic Commission's suspension of Ali's license "constituted an arbitrary and unreasonable departure for the commission's established practice of granting licenses to applicants convicted of crimes or military offenses." Thus, Ali could once again apply for a boxing license in New York.

Ali's exile from the ring officially was over, even though his pending legal problems would not be settled until June 1971. Typical of Ali's unpredictable nature was his reaction to the news that he could return to the ring.

"I don't have hard feelings against nobody," he said. "They did what they thought was right, and I did what I thought was right."

FIGHT OF THE CENTURY

CHAPTER 9

No longer the speedster he was before his long stretch out of the ring, Ali wound up in a slugfest against Joe Frazier March 8, 1971, at Madison Square Garden. This right to the head was one of several big shots landed by Frazier, who retained his heavyweight title with a unanimous 15-round decision.

Ali had hoped his October 26, 1970, return to the ring against Jerry Quarry might last longer than three rounds so that he could work on his stamina. However, showing the fast hands and quick feet that set the former champion apart, Ali quickly peppered his foe into submission. He caused a gash above Quarry's left eye and rendered him incapable of answering the fourth-round bell.

FIGHT OF THE CENTURY

Georgia Governor Lester Maddox, shown here signing a "Pickrick Drumstick" ax handle, was a strong opponent of integration—and of Ali resuming his boxing career in his state in 1970. He proclaimed the date of the Ali-Jerry Quarry bout a "Day of Mourning," and he said he hoped the former champ would be flattened in Round 1. Ali took the high road and ignored the opposition.

Joe Frazier sat on the horizon, just out of Muhammad Ali's reach. Frazier held the title belt declaring him heavyweight champion of the world, but Ali—the deposed "greatest"—remained the people's champion. A meeting between the two had to happen, as the entire boxing world longed for the matchup. But first, Ali needed to tend to other matters.

After three years away from the sport, a return to the ring was no small undertaking. Ali needed to knock off some of the rust before stepping into the ring with Frazier. While his body needed to be reconditioned, Ali's famed tongue and quick wit had not been affected by the layoff.

On September 10, 1970, Ali and Jerry Quarry attended a news conference at the Hotel Brookshire in Manhattan, where they signed a contract to meet in a 15-round fight at the Atlanta Auditorium on October 26, 1970. During this occasion, reporters asked Ali if the bout would be considered of championship ilk since Ali had been stripped of his title.

"This is for the championship of the whole world, the championship that's recognized by the people," Ali said.

Ali's comment served as the kickoff to months of verbal attacks against Frazier. Muhammad's verbal sparring also reminded

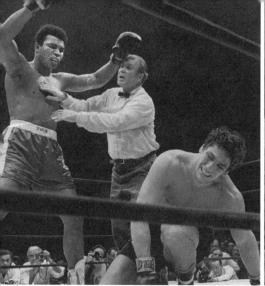

America what it had been missing during his absence: color. Ali's 10 championship fights had brought mixed reviews in ring stature, but the buildup to those bouts was another matter altogether. Ali always brought his "A" game when carving out a slice of prefight hype.

Georgia Governor Lester Maddox was among those displeased with Ali fighting in Atlanta. Elected governor in 1966 because of his strong stance against integration, Maddox issued a proclamation declaring October 26 a "Day of Mourning." He urged citizens of Atlanta to boycott the fight, and he deliberately referred to Ali as Cassius Clay. "I would hope that Clay gets beat in the first round and that he's flattened for a count of 30," Maddox said.

Ali ignored Maddox and noted: "When the fight was signed, people said, 'Are you gonna fight in Georgia? Are you gonna fight in Lester Maddox's state?' But I haven't had no trouble. Everybody calls me 'Champ,' they wave to me. Everything has been professional."

Typifying Ali's charm was the day he met Quarry's mother and wife. Ali told the mother: "You can't be Jerry's momma. You too young to be a grandmother. I don't believe it." And to his wife: "Jerry's wife? My, oh my. You are pretty. Don't know how Jerry's gonna train and stay away from you."

Ali scored a relatively easy third-round knockout over Quarry, displaying some of the quickness and footwork that separated him from other heavyweights. Ali had hoped the bout would last longer to build up his stamina, but the fight served as a way station he had to pass en route to fighting Frazier.

Ali wanted Frazier, and Smokin' Joe wanted Ali. After the Quarry fight, Frazier's manager, Yank Durham, told a *New York Times* reporter in a phone interview that Frazier wanted to fight Ali as soon as possible. Durham was with Frazier at Echo Lake, Pennsylvania, where he was training for a fight with Bob Foster. They did not see the Ali fight via closed-circuit television, but they had someone phone in the details. Durham gave his take on the fight, noting, "From what I heard, I wasn't impressed with the things he did." And when asked about Frazier's reaction, Durham offered: "He went to sleep."

Ali continued to tout himself to reporters the day after the Quarry fight. "I have the title now," he told a news conference. "Joe Frazier would like to fight me to be recognized by the people. Joe Frazier's just another contender now that I have a license."

Ali went on to praise Quarry at Frazier's expense, calling Quarry "a boxer and a puncher" while "Frazier's just one style, just a roundhouse puncher." He added: "I could

just jab and box him all night. Jab him, jab him, and when he gets close, tie him up, don't box close to him. Frazier would be three times easier to hit than Quarry."

Ali pointed out that Frazier needed seven rounds to beat Quarry while he had done the deed in three. "What prestige can I get from beating Frazier?" Ali said. "Technically he's the champion, but technical stuff don't mean too much in this country. People rebel against technical stuff. That's just a name, 'Joe Frazier the champion.' I've got the title now that I'm boxing again."

When and if the fight did come to being, Ali said he wouldn't even care if Frazier got billed as the champ. "No," he said with a smile. "After a few minutes, that would be determined. To those who might want it, the fight will come. All those Jewish promoters, they'll see that it comes off."

Madison Square Garden and the Houston Astrodome were the initial front-runners to host an Ali-Frazier fight, with a date to be determined. The Garden had forever been the king of venues for hosting big-time sporting events, but the Astrodome had an enormous capacity and a Texas-sized swagger of the future.

On November 5, 1970, Ali signed a contract to fight Oscar Bonavena at Madison Square Garden on December 7. Ali, the unquestioned master of spin, immediately began to hype the fight at the news conference, touting how tough Bonavena was going to be to beat. "He'll be much rougher than Jerry Quarry," he said. "Much rougher than George Chuvalo. Much rougher than Karl Mildenberger. Much rougher than Zora Folley." He explained: "Because he whipped all of them. He went 25 rounds with Joe Frazier, too. Had him down twice. He's tougher

Opposite left: Oscar Bonavena was no pushover, and Ali knew it. Calling his December 7, 1970, opponent "tougher than Frazier," Ali entered the Madison Square Garden ring expecting a battle in his effort to become the first fighter to knock out Bonavena. In the 15th round of a fight in which Ali showed plenty of rust, he did kayo Bonavena—and celebrated with raised gloves.

Opposite right: Stopping the "Louisville Lip" from talking was no easy task, particularly when the subject was Joe Frazier. On the penultimate day of 1970, as Frazier signed an agreement to fight Ali on March 8 in New York, the champion did the only thing he could think of in an effort to keep Ali from stealing the show. He was unsuccessful.

Above left: Though Ali trained amid fanfare in Miami Beach and Joe Frazier worked in a more low-key setting in Philadelphia for their 1971 bout, the press descended on Frazier's camp when Ali paid a loud visit on January 28. The two combatants also spoke on the telephone the night before the fight.

Above right: The stars were out March 8, 1971, when Ali and Joe Frazier fought at Madison Square Garden. In addition to Frank Sinatra, who was sizing up a photo opportunity ringside, the crowd included Woody Allen, Diana Ross, Sammy Davis, Jr., Hugh Hefner, Barbra Streisand, and Bill Cosby.

than Frazier. Hit him with every punch in the book." Holding his hands wide, he said, "Frazier's head was swollen this big."

"This is no tune-up for Frazier," Ali continued. "This is a real serious fight. A big one. If I lose, I lose everything."

Bonavena did not impress Frazier, who said of the Ali fight: "Oscar Bonavena couldn't hit Clay with a 30-30 rifle. If he hits Clay once all night, it's because Clay wants to be touched up to get his body in shape for me."

In the meantime, Frazier's title fight against Bob Foster on November 18 lost its sheen due to Ali's return to the sport. Frazier knocked out Foster, but Ali grabbed the headlines when he took to the podium—or assumed his own podium. While watching the fight via closed-circuit television in the Atlanta City Auditorium, Ali jumped up after Frazier's win and told the audience: "I want Joe Frazier. I want Joe Frazier."

Ali conducted his unique form of stand-up while shadow boxing. "Is Joe Frazier this fast? Can he do anything about this?" Ali said. "I won't have any trouble with Joe Frazier. I'll show him who the heavyweight champion of the world is. He never fought anybody. Bobby Foster is skinny, and that's the kind of people he has been fighting."

After the bout, Frazier responded to Ali's antics. "He talks loud because he's scared," Frazier said. "He needs me. I don't need him. He has to come to me."

Frazier even suggested indifference about fighting Ali. "I've got this job for money," Frazier said. "If I fight two other guys, I might make as much as I would fighting him. If it never comes off, I won't mope around. I'll just pick up and fight somebody else. If it's him, I'll beat him."

While Ali did not fulfill his prediction that Bonavena "will be mine in nine," he took

> "My mission is to bring freedom to 30 million black people. I'll win this fight because I have a cause. Frazier has no cause."
> —ALI

care of business by knocking him out in the 15th and final round. Though Ali won the fight—and became the first to knock out Bonavena—he looked rusty, prompting some to question whether he would be ready for a fight with Frazier.

Ferdie Pacheco, known as the "Fight Doctor," believed a meeting with Frazier was premature. "I felt that Ali's body had not achieved the hardness of the pre-exile years," he wrote in *Muhammad Ali: A View from the Corner*. "Some things might never be as they had been. Ali was not as fast, for example, and he could not 'dance all night long.'"

Ali looked different, too. He had gained 10 to 15 pounds and added 1½ inches around his biceps. The once tapered waist had grown thicker as well. Ali scoffed at the idea that he had grown rusty during his time away from the ring. He maintained that he had not lost anything; he simply fought differently than he once had, which could be seen in the Quarry and Bonavena fights. He did not dance as much. Instead, he used his balance to set himself to throw starch-filled punches, which reflected the transition of his body into more of a classic heavyweight.

The Houston Astrodome desperately wanted to book Frazier vs. Ali, which was hyped as the "Fight of the Century." The stadium could seat 60,000 for such an event. On December 10, Houston took a major step toward staging the fight when Astrodome Championship Enterprises filed for a Texas state boxing license on behalf of Ali, and the license was granted.

However, Madison Square Garden wasn't about to get beat out for this epic sporting event. And on December 30, 1970, at Toots Shor's Restaurant, the announcement was made that Ali and Frazier had agreed to face each other for the world

heavyweight championship fight on March 8, 1971, at the Garden. Each fighter received $2.5 million, a kingly sum at the time. Jack Kent Cooke, owner of the NBA's Los Angeles Lakers and the NHL's Los Angeles Kings, guaranteed the payouts with a Chase Manhattan Bank letter of credit. "The fight is the greatest entertainment and sports spectacle of all time," Cooke said at the news conference.

Jerry Perenchio, the president of Chartwell Artists, who promoted the fight in conjunction with Madison Square Garden, approached 70 possible backers before Cooke came through with the bulk of the purse money. Perenchio estimated that $20 million to $30 million would be made from the fight, prompting Ali to chortle: "They got us cheap, only five million out of 20 to 30. We've been taken."

Money wasn't the only subject on Ali's agenda that day. With Frazier sitting within arm's length of him, Ali called Frazier a "pretender to my throne." Muhammad made the promise that if Frazier somehow managed to win, he would crawl on his knees to Joe after the fight and hail him as "the greatest."

Frazier had knocked out 23 opponents while compiling a 26-0 professional record. Ali had accrued 25 KOs while running his professional record to 31-0. The fight would be the first in boxing history in which an unbeaten reigning heavyweight champion fought against an unbeaten former heavyweight champion.

Generally speaking, each fighter represented a distinct stereotype; thus, polarized factions followed both. Frazier had the earnest appeal of a hard-working, blue-collar, gospel-singing Baptist. Everything about him suggested that he was a no-nonsense man of integrity, from his forthright personality to his brawling, slug-it-out style in the ring. Frazier reluctantly became white America's hero, the force to stop everything they were afraid of in a changing society represented by Ali.

Ali remained the draft-dodging Black Muslim and an icon for black America. Many Americans considered him irreverent, cocky, and unwilling to take a backseat to anyone because of his color. Though both fighters trained hard, Frazier did so with little fanfare in a Philadelphia gym while Ali entertained his daily entourage while training in the Fifth Street Gymnasium in Miami.

Without all the window dressing, the bare bones of the fight set up to be a contest of two willful men with distinctly different boxing styles. Ali continued to exploit the division between the two fighters.

"I'm not just fightin' one man," Ali told *Time*. "I'm fightin' a lot of men, showin' a lot of 'em here is one man they couldn't conquer. My mission is to bring freedom to 30 million black people. I'll win this fight because I have a cause. Frazier has no cause. He's in it for the money alone."

Frazier resented how Ali orchestrated the public perception of him. In his autobiography, *Smokin' Joe*, Frazier wrote: "Clay was still trashing me as a Tom, and finding an audience for it. *Jet* magazine referred to me as 'the unheralded white-created champion for the primary enrichment of two white businessmen: Jack Kent Cooke and Jerry Perenchio.' What horseshit. As if Clay was going to put his two-point-five in the black community."

Heading into the fight, Ali was temporarily suspended from the Muslims, a sentence imposed due to Ali's alleged dependence on the white man's money rather than Allah. The measure did little to rock Ali's faith or his mental warfare against Frazier, which he carried out until the fight.

Frazier kicked back at New York's City Squire Hotel at 7th Avenue and 52nd Street the night before the fight, watching TV when his telephone rang. Ali wanted to talk to him.

"Joe Frazier, you ready?" Ali asked.

"I'm ready, brother," Frazier said.

"I'm ready, too, Joe Frazier. And you can't beat me. 'Cause I am the greatest."

"You know what?" Frazier said. "You preach you're one of God's men. Well, we'll see whose corner the Lord will be in."

"You sure you're not scared, Joe Frazier?"

"Scared of what I'm going to do to you."

"Ain't nothing you can do. 'Cause I'll be packing and poking and pouring water on your smokin'. Bye, Joe Frazier. See you tomorrow night."

"I'll be there," Frazier said. "Don't be late."

Angelo Dundee trained many fighters and normally wore the same white sweater into the ring for all of their fights. Ali wore red, so Dundee and the rest of Ali's entourage were given red sweaters with

> "Ain't nothing you can do. 'Cause I'll be packing and poking and pouring water on your smokin'. Bye, Joe Frazier. See you tomorrow night."
>
> —ALI, in a phone conversation with Frazier on the night before the fight

"Ali" on the back. Never one to allow superstitions to interfere with his business, Dundee reluctantly wore the red. Meanwhile, Ali predicted a sixth-round knockout.

Madison Square Garden drew worldwide attention on the night of the fight. Extra police were stationed in every corner, while celebrities moved about the premises. Woody Allen, Diana Ross, Sammy Davis, Jr., Hugh Hefner, Barbra Streisand, and Bill Cosby witnessed the spectacle. Noted author Norman Mailer was there to write an article for *Life* magazine, a story that would be accompanied by photographs shot by photography buff Frank Sinatra.

The Garden hosted a crowd of 20,455—generating a live gate of $1.3 million—while an estimated 300 million people worldwide watched the bout via closed-circuit TV.

What had only been hinted at before the fight quickly became evident in the first round: Ali no longer could dance and flick his quick hands like he once did. The modified Ali still could move, and the hands were quicker than most, but the battle would be waged more as one between two sluggers rather than one between fighters with contrasting styles.

From the outset, the fight went at a furious pace. The first three rounds belonged to Ali, but Frazier bloodied Muhammad's nose with a left hook in the fourth round and Ali began to show wear after the sixth, the round he had forecast would be the last. During the sixth, Frazier trapped Ali with his back to the ropes, landing shots to the former champion's body and head. Ali had a nice rally in the ninth. Attacking with left-right combinations, he seemed to be telling Frazier that if he was going to take his first professional defeat, he planned to die hard.

Through 10 rounds, the fight looked like a draw. Frazier then seized an opportunity with 49 seconds remaining in the 11th. Ali painted himself into a corner with no escape, and Frazier attacked with a hook that clearly hurt Ali. Another hook quickly followed, and Ali's legs turned to Jell-O. After falling into the ropes, Muhammad staggered away from Frazier, who knew he had hurt his opponent and wanted to finish the job. Somehow, Ali managed to finish the round.

Frazier capitalized on the momentum garnered from the 11th round to win the final four rounds. Sixteen seconds into the 15th, Frazier unleashed a left hook that sent Ali to the canvas. Again, the relentless Frazier tried to put him away. And once again, Ali's survival instincts kicked into high gear, allowing him to win a small battle of pride by finishing the round.

Alas, Ali lost the war. Frazier took a unanimous decision, and Ali had his first professional loss.

"That man can sure take some punches," Frazier said. "I went to the country, back home, for some of the shots I hit him with."

Ali did not address the media after the fight. Instead, he was hustled off to Flower-Fifth Avenue Hospital to have his swollen right jaw x-rayed. When he spoke the next day from a hospital bed, he waxed philosophically.

"It's a good feeling to lose," he said. "The people who follow you are going to lose, too. You got to set an example of how to lose. This way they can see how I lose. It'll be old news a week from now. Plane crashes, a president assassinated, a civil-rights leader assassinated, people forget in two weeks. Old news."

Though Ali lost the fight, he felt that the evidence of the fight indicated otherwise. "When I heard the decision, I had no feeling," he said. "Just go home, we lost, that's all. I made a lot of people lose. I don't think I lost yet. Except for my bruised jaw, look at my face—not a scratch. Now go look at Frazier's face.

Handing Ali his first professional loss took some doing, and Joe Frazier celebrated his unanimous decision with manager Yancey Durham after the fight at Madison Square Garden. Frazier praised Ali for his ability to take a punch, saying he hit him with all he had. The next day, Ali said he thought he had won nine of the 15 rounds.

"I know I won the most rounds; I think I won nine rounds. I caught a few shots, and the knockdown made it exaggerating. He numbed me a couple of times, but I won the most rounds. I hit him with everything and I couldn't put him down, but I know I hit him with more punches—three to one, without exaggeration. I know that. But the next time, no clowning. I never ran more than three miles a day for this fight. I should've done six. The people wore me out; couldn't go in the streets."

Ali refused to apologize after the fight, even though Frazier thought he should for the insults he had shelled out before the bout. "I'm not going to apologize to him," Ali said. "I know he said that I told him, 'I'm going to kill you, nigger,' but that's just ghetto talk."

Ali called Frazier "strong" and "good at his style." "He keeps coming, boy," Ali said. "But a man with his style won't be in boxing long. One thing I'm happy about, everybody got their money's worth. The crowd was pleased, that's the main thing. And if it wasn't for this jaw, I look good."

THE PEOPLE'S
CHAMP

CHAPTER 10

Light-heavyweight champion Bob
Foster left Ali cut and bruised for the
first time in his career on November 22,
1972, in Stateline, Nevada. However,
Foster also spent much of the fight
listening to referee Mills Lane count
while Ali stood in a corner. The final
knockdown came in the eighth round,
when Foster was unable to continue.

THE PEOPLE'S CHAMP

Though he seemed to go easy at times on Jimmy Ellis, his former sparring partner, during their July 26, 1971, fight in Houston, Ali did send Ellis reeling with a hard right in the fourth round. Ali hit Ellis with many quick shots before referee Jay Edson stopped the fight with 50 seconds remaining in the 12th round. Ali was back in the win column less than five months after his first professional loss.

Following his March 8, 1971, loss to Joe Frazier at Madison Square Garden, Muhammad Ali was more determined than ever to climb back to the top of the heavyweight division. He did not even need to step into the ring to declare his first victory in that quest. The triumph was, perhaps, the most important of his career.

On June 28, the U.S. Supreme Court ruled 8-0 to overturn Ali's 1967 draft evasion conviction. It could not be called a unanimous ruling, as Justice Thurgood Marshall abstained. Still, it provided long-awaited redemption for Ali, who had faced a possible five-year prison term, had been stripped of his belt, and had been out of boxing for three and a half years.

"Thanks to Allah," Ali said upon hearing the ruling. He then went on to explain why he felt people seemed to want to see him fail. "They're all afraid of me," he offered, "because I speak the truth that can set men free."

The Supreme Court upheld Ali's status as a conscientious objector to the Vietnam War based on his Black Muslim religious beliefs. En route to Ali's conviction, the Justice Department had advised selective service authorities that Ali's claim to be a conscientious objector was not valid since it did not satisfy any of the

Ali struck up a friendship with television sportscaster Howard Cosell over the course of his career. Here, he puts his own special touch on Cosell's hairstyle before the start of the U.S. Olympic boxing trials on August 7, 1972, in West Point, New York.

three required criteria: opposition to all wars; objection based on religious training; and sincerity.

The Supreme Court ruled that Ali's opposition was both sincere and based on religious training. Whether or not Ali was opposed to all wars was immaterial, the ruling stated, because the original conviction had been based on false information— "unlawful advice"—on the other two criteria. Ali, seemingly on the verge of serving jail time at several points over the previous four years, had been vindicated.

Some saw the ruling as being based on a very slight technicality. Others called it a slap in the face to all troops who had taken up the fight. "Like millions of other Americans," said Herbert C. Rainwater, Veterans of Foreign Wars commander-in-chief, "I am naturally very disappointed and embarrassed by the decision to reverse Cassius Clay's draft-evasion conviction. This is certain to have a demoralizing effect on our American men in uniform."

Others celebrated the decision. Upon hearing the ruling that morning, a black grocer in Chicago, who had just sold a glass of orange juice to Ali, dashed to catch up with the former champ and gave him the news. "I just heard on the radio," the man said, "the Supreme Court said you're free, an eight-to-nothing vote." Ali reportedly went back in and bought a round of orange juice for the house—a gathering of six or seven locals in the small shop. He then set out, with renewed vigor, to win back the title that had been taken from him.

Ali had been training to fight Jimmy Ellis on July 26 at the Houston Astrodome. It would mark the beginning of a 19-month run of 10 consecutive victories for a man who, in addition to calling himself "The Greatest," began touting himself as the "People's Champion."

Ellis was a former sparring partner for Ali, which might explain why Muhammad appeared less than enthused prior to the fight. He did not predict a round in which he would stop Ellis, and he admitted that he did not train like he would for a rematch with Frazier.

Ali, 31 pounds heavier than Ellis, moved well and peppered his overmatched foe for nearly the full 12 rounds, showing mercy at times when Ellis was in trouble. Referee Jay Edson finally stopped it with 50 seconds to go, awarding the bout to Ali on a TKO. After the fight, the Internal Revenue Service seized $130,000 as a tax pre-payment from Ali's $450,000 guarantee, a move Ali claimed

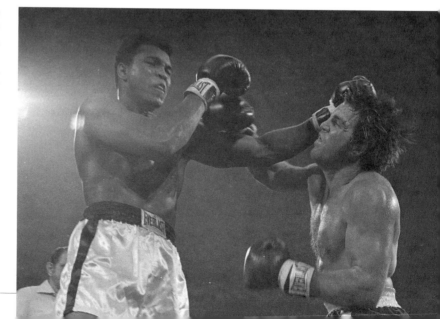

Ali had slimmed down to what he called his "dancing weight" for a June 27, 1972, rematch with Jerry Quarry in Las Vegas. The former champ, at 216 ½ pounds, did plenty of dancing and perhaps even more taunting, but it was a number of punishing blows like this straight left to Quarry's head that caused the fight to be stopped in the seventh round.

showed racial bias. "One little black boy makes a dollar, and he ain't going to be making it long," he said. "They won't let him use it."

If Ali was unusually quiet entering his bout with Ellis, the same was not true as he approached his November 17 matchup with Buster Mathis. Ali conceded that Mathis, who had gone 11 tough rounds with Frazier before being stopped, would not be a pushover. That, however, did not stop him from breaking out in rhyme the week of the fight. "Well, this is Buster's last stand," Ali told reporters. "I'll do to Buster what the Indians did to Custer."

It was not quite Little Bighorn, but Ali sent Mathis to the canvas four times—twice in each of the last two rounds. Mathis, 256 pounds and coming off a layoff of more than two years, did not have the legs or the skill to make it a match. Ali won in a unanimous decision. "I don't have it in my heart to hurt him with his wife and his little boy watching," Ali said. "The fight should've been stopped after the first knockdown. He had lost every round. I wasn't going to take the blame for killing him."

Though he lost two fights for the European heavyweight title, Jurgen Blin claimed to be the holder of that crown entering what most felt would be an international mismatch—him against Ali in Zurich, Switzerland, on the day after Christmas in 1971. Since the stocky West German spoke no English, American reporters did not press him on the issue. As it turned out, Blin proved to be a game competitor...until Ali landed a right cross in the seventh round that made the 28-year-old a knockout victim for the first time in his career.

Ali admitted that the crouching, charging Blin, fighting for a mere $45,000, hurt him twice. "He didn't have the skill," Ali said, "but he had the will, and sometimes the will can defeat the skill."

In March 1972, Ali arrived in Tokyo two weeks before an April Fool's Day fight with Mac Foster. He had a busy agenda. He said he planned to visit mainland China, learn karate, and knock out his foe in five rounds. His sightseeing and karate lessons panned out better than his prediction. Ali looked exasperated when Foster was standing after five. When he was still on his feet after 15, Ali—a unanimous winner by a wide margin—called him a great opponent. "Anyone who could last 15 rounds with me

> "Well, this is Buster's last stand. I'll do to Buster what the Indians did to Custer." —ALI, on Buster Mathis

Floyd Patterson hits the speed bag as Ali peers through an open window of his training camp in Deer Lake, Pennsylvania, on September 7, 1972. Ali had invited Patterson to help dedicate the new facility in advance of their fight, scheduled for two weeks later in New York. The extra workout did not keep Patterson from having his left eye closed by the quick hands of Ali, who won the fight by TKO.

Ali had to overcome a bad head cold and a controversial long count in the fifth round of what appeared to be an early knock-out of Al Lewis in Dublin on July 19, 1972. Lewis was allowed to continue, but Ali showed too much power. This left hook and several other big blows took their toll on Lewis, who was stopped in the 11th round.

"If you have anything you want to sell, have it printed on Chuvalo's heels and soles, because he shall fall."
—ALI, on George Chuvalo

must be great," said Ali, who landed jabs at will and was in control from start to finish.

Next on Ali's agenda was a 12-round rematch with George Chuvalo in Vancouver on May 1. Chuvalo, a veteran Canadian, had never been knocked down in a pro career that had spanned 86 fights entering this one. That did not keep Ali from predicting—with typical flair—that history was about to change. "If you have anything you want to sell," Ali shouted to promoter and Vancouver businessman Murray Pezim at a prefight press conference, "have it printed on Chuvalo's heels and soles, because he shall fall."

Ali put particular emphasis on uppercuts during sparring sessions, believing they would be key to knocking Chuvalo off his feet. Ali was impressive, bloodying Chuvalo's face with flurries of hard punches. The Canadian's sturdy legs held up again, but Ali won by unanimous decision, with one judge giving all 12 rounds to him. Chuvalo said he "enjoyed" the fight.

Ali faced a familiar opponent, Jerry Quarry, on a grander stage, Las Vegas, on June 27, 1972. Ali had cut Quarry badly two years earlier, stopping him in the third round of his comeback—Ali's first appearance in the ring since being stripped of his title in 1967. Uncut this time, Quarry lasted only until the seventh before succumbing to a

steady barrage of punches from a dominant Ali, who at 216½ pounds had returned to what he called his "dancing weight."

Ali was not only light on his feet—dancing and jabbing—he was also in top taunting form. He lowered his hands several times, daring Quarry to hit him. He bounced off the ropes and swiveled his hips. In the end, it was his sharp punches that brought the bout to an end 19 seconds into the seventh round.

"I'm back like I used to be, but better," said Ali, who after the victory declared himself ready for Frazier. "I'm stronger, smarter, hittin' better, movin', and I feel good."

Ali faced not Joe Frazier but Alvin Lewis in Dublin on July 19, 1972. Fighting for the fourth time in as many calendar months, Ali came down with a head cold that spanned the five days leading up to the bout— Ireland's first major professional prizefight in almost 40 years.

Ali's congestion did not affect the duration of the fight as much as a long count in the fifth round did. After Ali decked Lewis with a strong right hand, referee Lew Eskin made it to a count of nine when the bell rang. However, those in Ali's corner dubbed it a "22-second count." Lewis, 6'4" and awkward, recovered and fought gamely at times before his legs grew wobbly in the

11th round. That's when the referee called it off. "I was definitely weak," Ali said when asked about the cold. "I didn't have the zip to keep going."

Ali continued his heavy schedule, but he abandoned his fight-per-month pace to prepare for Floyd Patterson, the two-time former heavyweight champ whom he had stopped in 12 rounds in 1965. Their first fight had followed a war of words, largely focused on religious differences. By the rematch, Ali had developed a respect for his 37-year-old opponent who at one time had refused to call Ali by his Muslim name. This time there was no controversy. Ali, despite being an overwhelming favorite in the September 20 bout in New York, said he expected the match to go the full 15 rounds.

He was wrong. Ali played with Patterson through most of the first five rounds before unleashing a barrage of sixth-round punches that cut Patterson's left eyelid. The eye was virtually closed by the end of the seventh, and referee Arthur Mercante called the fight after a doctor's inspection.

Next up was Bob Foster in a fight staged in Stateline, Nevada, on November 21, 1972. Cut and bruised for the first time in his career, Ali bounced back to fulfill his prediction of an eighth-round knockout against the world light-heavyweight champion. Foster opened a cut over Ali's left eye and authored a purple bruise under it in the fourth and fifth rounds. Outweighed by more than 40 pounds,

however, he was not so adept at staying on his feet. Ali sent Foster to the canvas seven times, the final knockdown ending the affair 40 seconds into the eighth round. Asked about having his "pretty" face marked for the first time, Ali replied, "It's worth $250,000," his guaranteed cut of the purse.

Since falling to Frazier, Ali had defeated a West German and a Canadian, and he had fought in Switzerland, Japan, Canada, and Ireland. His 10th win in a row came against 22-year-old Joe Bugner—a Hungarian-born English citizen and the reigning European heavyweight champion. Their match was no honeymoon in Vegas, but it was staged in Sin City on Valentine's Day, 1973.

"Since when could a bug handle a bee," Ali recited in predicting a seventh-round knockout. "A bee that's as pretty and quick as me." Bugner sustained a cut over his left eye in the opening round but stayed on his feet all night. Though most agreed that the fight was not close, Ali's unanimous 12-round decision saw him prevail by only three points on two of the three scorecards.

In a whirlwind 19 months, Ali had improved his record by 10 wins to 41-1. He had boxed himself back into top form, and he had served notice that he was ready to avenge his defeat against Joe Frazier. First, however, the "People's Champion"—free from his legal concerns and focused squarely on regaining the title—had Ken Norton in his way.

"Since when could a bug handle a bee," Ali asked rhetorically before his Valentine's Day, 1973, bout with European heavyweight champion Joe Bugner in Las Vegas. However, Bugner did handle much of what Ali had to offer, including this right hand in the 10th round. Ali, who had predicted a seventh-round knockout, had to settle for a unanimous decision after 12 rounds.

JAWING WITH NORTON

Ali points to the jaw that Ken Norton broke during Norton's March 1973 victory in San Diego at a May 3 press conference that same year. The fighters were setting up a rematch—one that Ali, in typical fashion, predicted he would win with ease.

Ali planned to overpower Ken Norton in their March 1973 heavyweight fight in San Diego. Instead, he found himself covering up for much of the bout in an effort to protect a broken jaw he sustained from a Norton right hand early in the match.

JAWING WITH NORTON

Admittedly a little heavier than he would have liked to be entering their March 1973 fight, Ali said he would not have to be light on his feet to catch up with Norton. Fighting in his hometown of San Diego, Norton did have to duck and move to keep from being hammered by the former champion. However, he broke Ali's jaw in the early going and held on to take a narrow split decision.

There was considerable irony in the injury that led to Muhammad Ali's second career loss. Ken Norton, a heavyweight who had never fought a world-class fighter and was being paid a mere $50,000 to face Ali in his hometown of San Diego on March 31, 1973, landed a punch that broke Ali's jaw in the first round of the fight. Ironic, since it was Ali's jaw that had been taunting Norton in the weeks prior to the stunning upset.

A master of identifying an opponent's soft spot and turning it to mush, Ali had ridiculed Norton's reliance on a hypnotist for "the power of suggestion." Norton did not have enough power, Ali suggested. Muhammad entered the fight heavier than in past bouts at 221 pounds, but he shrugged off the extra mass in typical fashion. "A little heavy," he admitted, "but I don't have to be too fast for him."

Ali, whose only previous setback was the loss to Joe Frazier two years earlier, was a 5-1 favorite against Norton. Fans were clamoring for a rematch with Frazier. After Ali whipped Norton, they thought, that rematch would come.

Norton had other plans, and they did not include being an afterthought. Taking advantage of a more stationary Ali than earlier challengers had faced and moving easily himself, the

"Hometown Champ" caused what doctors called a "clean break" of Ali's jaw with an early overhand right. Ali's trainer, Angelo Dundee, said he wanted to stop the bout in the second round. A pained Ali would not let him.

The ex-champ disguised the injury well throughout the fight, save for a trickle of blood from his mouth. There was not much he could do about that.

Ali trudged on, though he seemed sluggish throughout the match. Norton was more active, but he connected on less than 10 percent of the punches he threw. It was clear entering the 12th and final round that a clear-cut winner had not been determined, but Ali had nothing left. Norton landed some of his best punches in the last round, though none was punishing. There were no knockdowns in the fight.

The referee called Norton a 7-5 winner. One judge gave Norton a 5-4 edge, while the other favored Ali 6-5. Norton had earned a split decision by the narrowest of margins. As the upset winner celebrated, Ali was taken to a nearby hospital for surgery on his broken jaw.

"He was very fast with his hands," Norton described of Ali, "but afoot he wasn't. He didn't have a punch at all."

Dundee said it was remarkable that Ali finished the fight, adding that he thought the bout was even entering the final round. "He's a fantastically gutty human being," Dundee said of his fighter. "When you have a broken jaw and you throw a punch, it hurts. When you get hit in the shoulder, it aches."

Weeks after the surgery, Ali's jaw was recovering just fine. It was in such good shape by summer that, with a rematch against Norton set for September 10 in Los Angeles, the jaw was back to touting its owner as "The Greatest."

It was an interesting summer for both fighters. Norton had a falling-out with his

> "Musically speaking, if he don't C sharp, he's gonna B flat."
> —ALI, on Ken Norton

hypnotist, Michael Dean, whom he had previously credited with helping instill a "killer instinct" in him before the first bout. Instead, Norton turned to studying "philosophies of success." He put himself through mind drills during breaks between workouts, building on the positive-thinking techniques that Dr. Dean had stressed.

Meanwhile, some were urging Ali to go into hiding after his Cherry Hill, New Jersey, neighbor, Major B. Coxson, was shot and killed execution-style with his stepdaughter in early June. The murder was linked to the "Black Mafia," and Ali was offered protection from the Philadelphia police. He refused it, calling Coxson—a onetime Camden, New Jersey, mayoral candidate, entrepreneur, and narcotics broker—a "good associate," but stressing his complete separation from the tragic events in his neighborhood.

"There's only one contract out for me, and that belongs to Ken Norton for our fight," Ali told *The New York Times* when asked if he was afraid for his life. "And I've got one out for him, too."

Two weeks later, Ali was shaking hands, kissing babies, and, of course, proclaiming his ring superiority with a smile during a tour of New York City. Fans flocked to watch the former champ playfully spar with members of the crowd. Some held posters promoting the upcoming rematch with Norton as the "Battle of Broken Jaw." Ali, back in his comfort zone after the injury, the loss, and some long days, basked in the spotlight. Throwing verbal barbs at Norton seemed like second nature.

"I had a broken jaw, too much weight, and a bad ankle," he told *The New York Times,* vowing to be at least 10 pounds lighter for the rematch. "But him, he did his best and all he got was a split decision. Musically speaking, if he don't C sharp, he's gonna B flat."

Opponents became accustomed to this view of Ali, who used his jab as well as any fighter in the world. This photo was taken during a 1973 interview in Philadelphia in which the 31-year-old ex-champ discussed his desire to regain the heavyweight title and return to preaching Islam.

It was vintage Ali. He belittled heavyweight champion George Foreman, calling him "the new tramp…er, champ." He saw a film marquee promoting *Tom Sawyer* and asked, "Who did Tom Sawyer ever whup?" He said he was "intoxicated with greatness." His adoring fans ate it up.

Red Smith, the famed New York sportswriter, warned that Ali's overconfidence could again haunt him. Ali, Smith noted, already had plans to begin work as a television boxing analyst just three weeks after the fight—a role that would require his jaw to be in working condition at the time. Smith pointed out that Ali's doctors and handlers had been advising him to keep his teeth clenched around his mouthpiece in the ring, a style that would be difficult to follow for a man accustomed to taunting his opponent. However the second Ali-Norton fight played out, one thing was certain.

The world would be watching.

Ali weighed in at 212, nine pounds lighter than in the first fight and seven pounds heavier than Norton. Ali was installed as a 12-5 favorite for the bout at the Forum in Inglewood, California, meaning Norton's earlier win had garnered at least a few believers.

"I plan on fighting George Foreman as soon as I can get him," said Norton, who was guaranteed $200,000 for the rematch, compared to a $275,000 guarantee for his better-known opponent.

"This time I'm 100 percent right," Ali countered, convinced that he was his own worst enemy in the spring loss. "Same Norton. No contest."

Ali's prediction looked accurate for six rounds of the 12-round match. Though he did not employ the "Ali Shuffle" or "rope-a-dope" or any of his other tricks, his feet moved swiftly, his jabs landed accurately, and he fought with style and purpose. This was the Ali who his fans had come to expect. If he had not won all of the first six rounds, he certainly had taken most of them. If he could keep up the pace, surely Norton would absorb one too many blows and hit the canvas in the later rounds.

However, an injury again stood in Ali's path. Pain shot through his right hand after he landed a sixth-round punch. He thought it might be broken. Then suddenly, the momentum took a dramatic turn. Ali tired, and he became flat-footed. His jabs were neither as sharp nor as forceful. Norton sensed the change and began to pressure his opponent. Round 7 was his. Then 8 and 9. Then 10 and 11.

Entering the final round, the rematch shaped up much like the first bout. Neither fighter had been knocked down. Both were being told in their corners that victory was up for grabs. Win the 12th round, and the fight was yours. This time, Ali had something left in reserve. Perhaps it was the result of his more rigorous training. Perhaps he simply willed himself back on his toes. Whatever the reason, Ali regained the bounce he had displayed in the early stages, and—even with weary punches—clearly won the final round.

"I knew if I closed the show," he said from a couch in his dressing room after the fight, "I'd stand a better chance of winning. I knew I had to move in for the attack. Jab, jab, move, move, then in again."

All three men responsible for scoring the bout gave the 12th round to Ali. On the referee's and one judge's scorecards, it made the difference in 6-5 and 7-5 margins for Ali. The other judge had Norton clinging to a 6-5 advantage. For the second straight time, Ali and Norton had battled to a split decision. This time, it was Ali celebrating, though relief might be a better description of his mood.

Norton protested. His punches were more forceful, he argued. Though most analysts agreed—and still do—with the judges that Ali won a close decision, Norton was not entirely alone in thinking that he had won the fight on the strength of his performance in the later rounds.

Don Fraser, who promoted the fight, told "Cyber Boxing Zone" years later that Ali's popularity may have worked to his advantage in that fight and others. "Norton won the first, and I think he won the second and third," Fraser said, referring to a September 28, 1976, bout at Yankee Stadium that made the Ali-Norton series one of boxing's best trilogies. "But I think when Ali got in the ring, he already had a couple of

rounds in his favor before he threw a punch, because he was Ali."

And because he was Ali, it was time to keep moving. In fact, there was no time to waste. Ali's camp was quick to announce that plans were in the works for the Ali-Frazier rematch that people longed to see—a fight that was expected to top their $20 million mega-bout of two years earlier. After a 1974 date was settled on and announced, Ali and Frazier took to shouting insults at each other at a Madison Square Garden news conference. Ali, to no one's surprise, seemed to get the better of his rival in the verbal department.

However, not everyone in the media was lauding Ali in the aftermath of his back-to-back struggles against Norton. Columnist Dave Anderson of *The New York Times* wrote that "The Greatest" had become "The Tiredest." Others wondered whether the

Opposite: Ali's second wife, Belinda, is surrounded by their children at her husband's training camp in Deer Lake, Pennsylvania, in August 1973. Muhammad Jr. *(in lap)*, Maryum *(standing)*, and twins Reesheda and Jamillah were among their father's biggest fans.

Ali was nine pounds lighter for his second bout with Ken Norton, and it showed in the early rounds of their September 10, 1973, battle in Inglewood, California. He was quick on his feet and landing punches seemingly at will before injuring his right hand when he landed a sixth-round blow. The former champ finished strong in the 12th round, however, and claimed a split decision.

former champion had enough energy left to reclaim the glory that had been his years earlier.

In late October, Ali canceled the remainder of an exhibition tour of the Far East. It was a tour he had planned before the rematch with Norton, and perhaps it seemed a fine idea at the time. A hard punch absorbed to the jaw by sparring partner Orlando Johnson during an exhibition bout in East Malaysia—and perhaps poor turnouts in Jakarta and Singapore—changed his mind. Ali returned to the United States, where he was to undergo a checkup.

Medically, Ali was fine. In fact, he was on the verge of what would turn out to be one of his greatest years in 1974. As 1973 came to a close, however, some speculated about whether Ali was prepared for a rematch with Frazier. Others wondered whether, should he ever meet Foreman, he could withstand the brute strength of the champ.

Yes, Ali's victory over Norton provided sweet revenge for the fast-talking "People's Champion." But the two hard-fought battles exposed the need for Ali to raise the level of his performance as he prepared to taunt and jab his way back to the top of the heavyweight division.

REVENGE IN THE GARDEN

CHAPTER 12

When Joe Frazier stepped up his attack in the late rounds, thinking he needed a knockout to win, Ali was up to the challenge. Using counterpunches like this left to the head late in the bout, Ali continued to capture rounds on the judges' scorecards to secure a unanimous decision.

REVENGE IN THE GARDEN

Five days before their January 1974 rematch at Madison Square Garden, a war of words broke out between Ali and Joe Frazier at a TV screening of their previous bout in an ABC studio. After Frazier mentioned that he had sent Ali to a hospital in their first fight, Ali called Frazier ignorant and the two wound up out of their seats in confrontation. Each was fined $5,000 by the New York State Athletic Commission.

That Muhammad Ali actually fought Rudi Lubbers speaks volumes about Ali. It says much about the way boxers approached their craft and the pride they took in the simple act of fighting. By today's soft and selfish standards, the Ali-Lubbers fight is difficult to fathom.

Just six weeks after beating Ken Norton in a hard-fought rematch, and with his second fight against Joe Frazier already signed, Ali climbed into the ring with Lubbers. The reigning champion of Holland was hardly on anyone's short list of great heavyweights, but he was not without merit. Lubbers had gone 15 rounds with Joe Bugner in a losing effort for the European heavyweight title. He would also twice beat Jean Pierre Coopman, who would later challenge Ali for the title.

In the current era of boxing, the superstars fight no more than twice a year. Promoters often require six months to build up interest in a fight. Ali, though, could generate the same level of hype with a single interview. Still, the Lubbers fight seemed unnecessary in any era. Why would Ali risk injury and jeopardize the Frazier rematch?

The answer is as simple as it is complex. Ali loved to fight. He loved the stage, the roar of the crowd, and the adrenaline rush of

John Kennedy, Jr., the son of late President John F. Kennedy and no stranger to famous photos, gives Ali a punch in the nose prior to Ali's January 1974 rematch with Frazier. Madison Square Garden was sold out for the event, and tickets were made available to watch the fight on closed-circuit television in the basement.

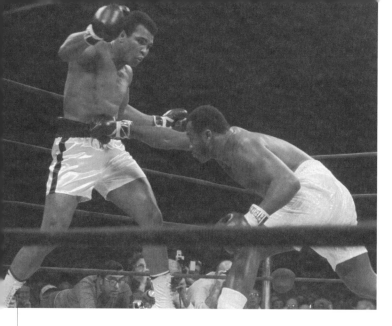

In a change of tactics from their first fight, Ali did not stand toe-to-toe with the hard-charging Frazier in their second meeting. When Frazier attacked, Ali slipped punches, counterpunched, or tied up his opponent.

"Only good boxers can be handsome because they don't get hit. It's the ugly boxers who are not good. Frazier is ugly. Foreman is ugly." —ALI

asserting his dominance upon an opponent. Ali always fought, even when he should have rested. The idea of fighting Lubbers in Jakarta, Indonesia, a largely Muslim country, also appealed to his sense of loyalty. It was a gift the former champion would give to his foreign fans.

On the eve of the bout, Ali was already thinking about his future. At the final prefight press conference, Muhammad lauded Lubbers' ability, but he also took the opportunity to engage in some psychological warfare with his favorite target. "I can see from his face how good he is," Ali said. "[Lubbbers] has to be good because he is handsome. I am handsome. Only good boxers can be handsome because they don't get hit. It's the ugly boxers who are not good. Frazier is ugly. Foreman is ugly."

Ali predicted Lubbers wouldn't last more than five rounds. They fought on October 20, 1973, inside the country's national soccer stadium. The stubborn Dutch heavyweight was bleeding from the nose and his right eye was swollen shut, but he remained upright until the final bell. After 12 rounds of catching leather, Lubbers wasn't so handsome. Ali was awarded a unanimous decision by the scores of 60-45, 60-42, and 59-52.

"Lubbers is a good fighter," Ali said after the match. "I hit him with everything I could."

If the action was lively, the gate was not. Hoping to draw on Ali's appeal in the Islamic world, promoters staged the fight in Senyan Stadium, an immense venue that could accommodate up to 120,000 fans. But the fight drew only 25,000. It would be the last time Ali would play to so many empty seats.

When a reporter asked Ali after the Lubbers fight why he didn't throw many rights hands, Ali made a fist and said, "I have to save this for Joe Frazier!"

Frazier would be ready, even if the rest of the world was not.

It was easy for the boxing press to dismiss the rematch between Ali and Frazier. Since their epic first encounter in 1971, both fighters looked to be mere mortals. Frazier had been dethroned as champion by George Foreman, who dropped Smokin' Joe six times en route to a humiliating second-round knockout. Meanwhile, Ali suffered a broken jaw while losing a split decision to the relatively unknown Norton. Both men were past their respective primes, a mantra the media repeated often.

"There wasn't the same atmosphere at the Garden as there was for the first fight," recalled Tom Kenville, who worked publicity for Madison Square Garden. "It wasn't as big an event. There was no world title on the line. There was a sense that both of them had slipped a little."

For the fighters, their intense dislike for one another had hardly waned. "If you've been around this guy long enough, you can have a lot of hate in your heart when the bell rings," Frazier told the press. "But otherwise you kind of look at him and you laugh. There's something wrong with this guy. I'm aware now that the guy has a couple of loose screws someplace."

One incident revived interest in the fight and took the rivalry to a new level. Both fighters appeared with Howard Cosell on ABC's *Wide World of Sports* five days before the rematch. The fighters were to review a tape of their first fight, with Cosell acting as a moderator. It was the first time that the "Fight of the Century" was shown on network television.

Frazier initially resisted the idea, having grown tired of Ali's histrionics. But Cosell guaranteed that the conversation would remain strictly on boxing. The flaw in the planning was that Cosell inexplicably did not sit between them. Frazier arrived on set last, taking a seat in the middle of Ali and Cosell. To the viewers at home, the seating arrangement was Ali to the right, Frazier center, and Cosell to the left. It was a lineup for disaster.

While Ali had been at his bombastic best throughout the promotion, it was Frazier who inadvertently incited a mini-riot on the set. During the broadcast, he casually mentioned that he had sent Ali to the hospital after the first fight. Reacting to Frazier's breech of the rules, Ali responded by calling Frazier ignorant. Frazier responded by rising from his chair and challenging Ali. Ali's brother, who had been standing off stage, walked menacingly to the set. "You want in on this, too?" asked Frazier, glaring at Rahman Ali.

Muhammad sensed the anger in Frazier, and in an attempt to defuse the situation, rose from his chair and bear-hugged his opponent. Frazier, who was seething, wrestled Ali to the ground. Both men were then separated. The rematch would still take

place in five days, but their behavior did not go unpunished. The New York State Athletic Commission fined the fighters $5,000 for "deplorable conduct demeaning to boxing."

The real fight was held on January 28, 1974, at Madison Square Garden. The arena had been sold out since January 17, but tickets were also available to watch the bout in the Garden's basement—the Felt Forum—on closed-circuit television. Ali, age 32, was a 6-5 betting favorite as he put his North American title on the line. Frazier, age 30, weighed in at 209, three and a half pounds heavier than when they fought the first time. By contrast, Ali weighed 212, three pounds lighter than when they met in 1971.

In the moments before the bell, Ali was far less defiant than in their first meeting. Ali typically used the prefight instructions as a stage to intimidate his opponent, but on this night—when the two boxers were ordered to the center of the ring by referee Tony Perez—Ali chose to look anywhere but at Frazier. While Smokin' Joe stared upward at his foe, Ali swiveled his head, surveying the Garden. He even looked over to the press section and winked.

"I wasn't at the Garden for the first fight, which was, of course, one of the greatest fights in history," said Bobby Cassidy, a light heavyweight contender who fought on the undercard of the rematch. "But let me tell you, the Garden was still electric for the rematch. No matter who they had lost to, this was still Muhammad Ali and Joe Frazier in that ring. And when they got into that ring, they didn't disappoint anyone."

This fight began where the first one left off. Frazier swarmed in behind a wrecking ball of a left hook. Ali peppered Frazier with jabs and chopping right hands. They set a furious pace, one befitting of a pair of middleweights.

Two controversies would forever hang over this fight. The first occurred in Round 2. Late in that round, Ali landed a blistering

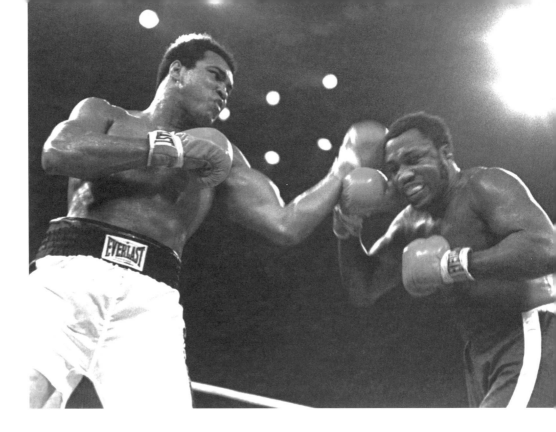

Although Ali was never able to knock Frazier off his feet, he did pepper his opponent with jabs and hooks throughout their second fight at Madison Square Garden. Ali had Frazier teetering on the ropes in the second round, but referee Tony Perez thought he heard a signal for the end of the round and kept Ali from pouring it on.

Opposite: Back at Madison Square Garden on the day after their fight in January 1974, Ali and a shades-wearing Frazier appeared to be on friendly terms. Ali had won a unanimous decision in their 12-round battle.

right cross that knocked Frazier back on his heels. As Frazier wobbled to the ropes, Ali moved in, only to be intercepted by the referee. Perez thought he had heard someone call "bell," and he moved in to end the round. When he realized his mistake, and called the fighters back together, Frazier had recovered. About 20 seconds remained in the round when the fighting resumed.

Frazier was indeed in trouble, but over the years the impact of the gaffe has grown out of proportion. Consider this: In 41 rounds of fighting, over three bouts, Ali never floored Frazier. It is highly unlikely that he would have done so in those final moments of Round 2.

The other controversy was subtle but more telling in the outcome of the bout. Frazier's camp complained throughout the 12 rounds and after the contest that Ali was able to get away with repeated holding. Their frustration was legitimate, but Ali did not violate any rules. He simply disrupted Frazier's rhythm by tying him up. That was

the primary difference between the first two fights. In the "Fight of the Century," Ali stood toe-to-toe with Frazier. In the rematch, if the heat became too much, Ali clinched. It was a smart tactic and certainly not illegal.

Still, Frazier had his moments. Ali found himself in trouble in the seventh round after a pair of sweeping left hooks backed him to a corner. Muhammad responded to adversity like he always had, by tapping into a seemingly endless reservoir of courage and determination. Frazier sensed that he needed a knockout to win the bout and pressed his attack in the second half. But Ali won Rounds 9 and 11 on all three of the judges' scorecards to secure the win.

"Let me tell you," Cassidy said, "they were perfect for each other. Their styles contrasted perfectly. If they fought 100 times, it would be the same fight and it would always be a great fight. Yes, I believe they genuinely didn't like each other, which helps fuel the intensity. But more than that, they were great fighters who didn't like to lose. They had tremendous pride in who they were and what they did. And when that bell rang, they left nothing behind."

The end result was a close but clear unanimous decision for Ali. The scoring by rounds was 7-4-1, 8-4, and 6-5-1. Each man was guaranteed $850,000 against 32.5 percent of the net income of the fight. When all the receipts were totaled, they each pocketed roughly $2.5 million—the same they made for their first fight. It would be the largest grossing non-world title heavyweight fight in history.

At the postfight press conference, Ali was gracious. It was not unusual for him, particularly if the bout was a tough battle, to compliment his opponent after a fight.

"I can't say nothing bad about him," Ali said. "I actually thought Joe was finished. He isn't. He had me out on my feet twice. There's no bad feeling between us. I'm gonna give Joe another chance. I'm not gonna duck him."

There would be a slight detour to Ali-Frazier III—one that would take Ali to Zaire and the top of the boxing world.

RUMBLE IN THE JUNGLE

CHAPTER 13

Fans in Kinshasa, Zaire, were eager to welcome Ali on September 17, 1974—six weeks before his fight there against heavyweight champion George Foreman. The bout had been scheduled for September 24, but it was rescheduled while Foreman recovered from a facial injury.

Fight promoter Don King addresses media members in Kinshasa while Ali, ready to battle Foreman for the heavyweight championship, works the head of cornerman Bundini Brown eight days before the 1974 match.

RUMBLE IN THE JUNGLE

A spear-wielding dancer in Zaire clears the way for Ali in September 1974 as the former heavyweight champ arrives for a fight with reigning champion George Foreman. Ali had chartered a plane from Paris for the fight, which was preceded by great fanfare in the Central African country.

Cassius Clay, circa 1964, might have been a little naive when it came to understanding the dangers of a mauler like Sonny Liston. Muhammad Ali, who at age 32 prepared to fight George Foreman, obviously had a better understanding of the task facing him. Older and wiser, Ali had to tap into a well of courage to take on the imposing Foreman, a foe who appeared capable not only of winning a fight, but also of inflicting physical damage while doing so.

Foreman had been a hero at the 1968 Olympics in Mexico City, winning a gold medal in the heavyweight division. He became a beloved patriotic figure in doing so, as he waved a small American flag after his final and deciding match. The muscular Texan ventured into the professional ranks shortly after the Olympics. He ripped through his opponents like a tornado through a trailer park to earn a title shot against Joe Frazier on January 22, 1973, in Kingston, Jamaica.

Frazier's brawling style had worked against Ali almost two years earlier. Yet when he went up against Foreman, his tactics failed miserably. Foreman destroyed the champion, knocking him down six times in two rounds before the fight ended at 1:35 of the second.

Ali had eyes and a brain. He understood that Foreman possessed a hefty bag of skills housed in a body chiseled by the boxing gods. Foreman had youth on his side as well.

Typical of Ali, he downplayed Foreman's win. He announced that he would be able to schedule a fight with Foreman in a year. He added confidently, "I know I would annihilate [Foreman]."

But one has to wonder how confident Ali was about beating Foreman, particularly in light of Foreman's two title defenses after putting away Frazier. The reigning champion easily dispatched Joe "King" Roman and Ken Norton, the latter of whom he finished off in two rounds. That meant that Foreman had needed less than four rounds to humiliate the two men who had defeated Ali—Frazier and Norton.

The numbers were chilling: In Foreman's three title fights, he put away Frazier, Roman, and Norton in 11 minutes and 35 seconds, spread over parts of five rounds. Nevertheless, Ali appeared confident.

"I don't have no fear of Foreman," Ali said. "Maybe that's why I been slipping, why I lost two fights. I take it too light. Fighting George Foreman is just another day in the gymnasium."

Foreman cut a young and cocksure figure at age 25. When asked early in 1974 if he wanted to fight Ali, the champion said he would fight him in Africa for $5 million, adding: "I would jump out of airplanes and fight 20 Alis for $5 million."

The fight was scheduled for a 3 A.M. start on September 25, 1974, in Kinshasa, Zaire, which had once been Leopoldville in the Belgian Congo. The early morning start allowed the fight to be aired at 10 P.M. Eastern Time in the United States. Each fighter would be paid $5 million. Reporters

"When all the brothers are out on the street, scuffling over some woman or over who shot the dice first or last, that is the punch they throw at three in the morning." —ALI, on his new punch, the "Ghetto Whopper"

noted that not only were both fighters black, but so was the fight's promoter (Don King) and the bout's referee (Zack Clayton). The host country also was predominantly black.

Ali began hyping the fight immediately. At the famed Rainbow Room in New York City, he conceded that he could not take anything away from what Foreman had already accomplished in the ring. He noted that Norton had broken his jaw in their first fight and he had escaped with a close decision in their second fight. But Ali still felt like he could win for three reasons. The first was the power of Allah. Ali noted that he felt as though he held a good standing with his god, whom he said controlled everything. Next, he cited his experience and how he planned to stay out of Foreman's way for as many as five rounds. What he noted third would prove prophetic.

"Three, you ain't seen George Foreman tired yet," Ali said. "Round 4, Round 7, Round 9, Round 13…last round. I haven't seen George in a good scuffle yet. I haven't seen him get winded."

Ali listed the likes of Liston, Frazier, Floyd Patterson, George Chuvalo, and Henry Cooper, saying each of his previous foes hit harder than Foreman, yet he won his fights. "And another thing, I don't eat pork," Ali said. "By me not eating pork, I don't think like pork eaters. I'm not an ordinary what you call Negro."

As for the 3 A.M. start to the fight, Ali said he planned to deal with the early start by employing a new punch. In entertaining fashion, he described to the audience what he called the "Ghetto Whopper"—a punch similar to former welterweight champion Kid Gavilan's famed "bolo punch." Ali credited Gavilan for teaching him the

Heavyweight champion George Foreman was younger (25) and more chiseled than Ali entering his October 1974 title defense in Zaire. Foreman, pictured here at the weigh-in for the bout, had knocked Joe Frazier to the canvas six times in two rounds—something Ali had failed to do even once in two previous fights.

Foreman's punches, including a left to the jaw that caused Ali to wince, packed plenty of pop. However, Ali worked his fight plan to perfection. Knowing that Foreman had rarely been tested in late rounds, he covered up and used the "rope-a-dope" tactic in the first half of the fight, allowing Foreman to wear himself out throwing punches that did not have their desired effect. Then Ali went to work.

punch. He then asked Gavilan to stand in the audience and demonstrate it, which he did.

Where did the "Ghetto Whopper" get its name? Ali explained that it was the kind of punch that is thrown in the ghetto at 3 A.M.

"When all the brothers are out on the street, scuffling over some woman or over who shot the dice first or last, that is the punch they throw at three in the morning," he said.

Ali added a touch of drama by hinting that the fight with Foreman might be his last.

Foreman could not possibly counter the quick-witted, prefight dialogue that would spew from his opponent's mouth during the months leading up to their fight. He came off as rather bland in comparison to the loquacious Ali. Yet through his almost stoic nature, Foreman appeared nearly indestructible. Ali did not register on his radar as a major threat.

During a tour of the United Nations, Foreman—the Olympic hero and a concerned humanitarian—observed many of the world's current events through the eyes of those at the UN and declared that he was a "citizen of the world." During this public appearance, Foreman also spoke of his upcoming fight, giving no indication that the former champion concerned him in the least.

After camping out on the ropes for much of the first six rounds in Zaire, covering his head and letting Foreman tire himself out throwing body shots, Ali began to unleash his own attack in the seventh. He pounded a weary Foreman with this right hand in the seventh. In the blink of an eye, Ali was in control of the bout.

"I like to think it will end pretty quick," Foreman said. "I don't like fights. I just land the right punch and everything is over. Nobody gets hurt and nobody gets killed."

In Zaire, preparations for the fight included a furious race to update the site of the fight. *Stade du 20 Mai*'s capacity was 35,080 when utilized for its normal use as a soccer stadium, but it would be expanded to seat 120,000 for the fight. Of those seats, 4,000 were earmarked to be ringside at $250 a pop. The TV audience for the fight was expected to be enormous. Simply stated, Ali-Foreman was the biggest event to ever come to the copper-rich Central African nation. To the citizens and government of Zaire, the fight afforded them the opportunity to show the rest of the world that they were not a Third World country, but rather a developing nation.

Clearly, Ali reigned as the favorite among the people. A poll by *Elima,* a daily newspaper, revealed that Ali was "favored" by approximately 75 percent of the survey sample. Most of this popularity could be attributed to the simple fact that he had been around longer and had attained a worldwide celebrity due to his politics and his prolonged exile from the ring. Yet Ali stirred the pot like he had so many times prior to other big fights. He portrayed himself as the persecuted black man returning to the country of his roots. Such depictions by Ali always cast his opponent in an adversarial light by creating the appearance of a racial divide. He called Foreman's flag waving at the Olympics "Uncle Tomism" and gave him the nickname "The Mummy."

However, when Ali prompted his fans to employ Foreman voodoo dolls—and when he created the imagery of Foreman being stuck to a pot of boiling water—few were amused. In fact, it was counter to everything Zaire leaders tried to depict about their nation. Promoters of the event also disapproved of Ali's creation of where the fight would take place. They believed Ali's myth about Zaire, as a land of spear-carrying Tarzan extras, would drive away Americans from traveling to the fight. Don King noted: "This talk about the rumble in the jungle and voodoo dolls looking like George Foreman—why, it would scare me away."

In early September 1974, famed daredevil Evel Knievel made his much-ballyhooed attempt to leap over the Snake River Canyon in a rocket-powered motorcycle. Just prior to shipping off for Africa

"If Evel Knievel can make that jump, I can whip Foreman's rump.... Oh, George, you are going to be in trouble, big trouble." —ALI

While Ali stepped back in the eighth round, Zack Clayton did something no other referee had done. He counted George Foreman out. Foreman had won all of his 40 previous bouts—37 by knockout—before succumbing to Ali's skill and strategy in the Zaire classic that became known as the "Rumble in the Jungle."

for the fight, Ali made a public appearance in the Empire Room of the Waldorf-Astoria in New York City and incorporated Knievel's attempt into his dialogue about winning his upcoming fight.

"If Evel Knievel can make that jump, I can whip Foreman's rump," Ali said. "It is befitting that I leave just like I came in, beating a big bad man who can't be beat, like I did Sonny Liston just 10 years ago…. I'm looking good. I'll be 213. Oh, George, you are going to be in trouble, big trouble."

Complications for the fight arose on September 17 due to a heavyweight named Bill McMurray. Serving as a sparring partner to Foreman, the 28-year-old from Sacramento landed a punch to the area between Foreman's right eye and eyebrow, opening a long gash and causing the postponement of the fight. The bout, which had been scheduled for September 25, now hung in limbo until it could be rescheduled for a later date.

Ali seemed particularly downtrodden about the news, noting that he felt like "somebody close to me just died." He thought of the financial repercussions, calling the injury a "$50 million cut."

Several days later, the fight was rescheduled for October 29. Ali remained skeptical of the rescheduling. A cut to the face is a serious matter for any fighter. Healing is not an easy process, and on top of that, a fighter

can't do much actual training in the ring while waiting for the injury to heal. Judging the risk, Ali felt as though the fight would be rescheduled again, perhaps as late as three months after the injury.

But Foreman did not proceed cautiously, and he adhered to the October 29 date. In doing so, he said, he gave in to the pressure of the event. He noted the efforts of promoter friends and acquaintances who had worked hard to sell tickets.

With the fight drawing near, Ali added a healthy dose of P. T. Barnum. During a 25-minute TV linkup from Zaire, he told the audience about his future plans: "I plan to retire as soon as I win; there won't be no lose." He continued to belittle Foreman by noting that the champion was doing all he could to get out of the fight, but he would not be able to do so, adding: "When I beat him, I want to be acclaimed as the greatest fighter of all time."

Two days later, he built up the fight to epic proportions, calling it "the biggest event in the history of the world since the Roman gladiators." And when asked if he had a prediction, he responded: "I'm a wonder. The fifth wonder of the world. I'm faster than Muhammad Ali. I'm going to knock him out in three…two…one."

Foreman's rhetoric paled in comparison: "I'll be doing my 100 percent best. That's my only prediction."

Ali dedicated the fight to all the African people who he said were fighting for their freedom. He said he looked at Foreman as a Belgian, which in his mind meant an oppressor of all black nations. He also declared the fight a Holy War, and that the powers that had worked for him in the past would help him prevail.

Foreman never truly engaged in any give and take with Ali, but Dick Stadler, his manager, said the fight would be Foreman's easiest. He added that if he didn't win, it would be because of something Foreman neglected to do rather than something Ali did. Sadler said Foreman would not make the mistake of chasing Ali, like other fighters had, and that Foreman was just a better fighter. He could punch better, he was as fast as Ali, and he was better to the body. He summed up his comments by saying: "I don't see what can make it hard for him."

On the morning of the fight, Ali entered the grand stage dressed in a white satin robe with a trim that resembled an African blanket. He then spent approximately 10 minutes dancing and shadow boxing in the ring to the crowd's approval. Foreman then entered the ring wearing a red velvet robe with a blue sash.

From the beginning, Foreman appeared eager to put away Ali early. In the first round, he trapped Muhammad against the ropes and unleashed a medley of punches against his ribs. When the bell rang to end the round, Ali returned to his corner, took a seat on a stool, and winked to the camera.

"He hits hard, but not so hard that I can't take it," Ali told his corner. "Liston hit harder. It's hot out there. It's muggy. Hard to breathe."

Ali threw a series of combinations in the second round. In the third, he returned to the ropes, allowing Foreman to wale away at him. (A few months later, Ali would dub this tactic the "rope-a-dope.") After the third round, Ali chose to stand in his corner and mug for the ringside cameras rather than take a seat. In the fourth, Ali jabbed at Foreman's head at the beginning of the round before settling into the ropes again like a house cat on a La-Z-Boy. Also during the fourth, Foreman looked tired for the first time, walking after Ali rather than chasing him. Foreman did not have to chase his foe in the fifth because Ali covered up for most of the round, content to let Foreman punch away.

During the period between the fifth and sixth rounds, an official appeared to loosen the ropes. Ali's trainer, Angelo Dundee, had actually tightened the ropes at 4 P.M. on the previous day, but the heat extracted much of the tightness by the next day's 4 A.M. start, leaving the ropes loose.

Ali's tactic of letting Foreman pound away at his body while he covered his head did not sit well with Dundee. Each time Ali returned to the corner, Dundee told him to take the fight to Foreman and not allow himself to get beaten to a pulp while covering up in the corner. Each time that Dundee offered his comments, Ali retorted that he knew what he was doing. Dundee was not convinced. One time, he even hit Ali on his backside to get him off the ropes.

After the fight, Ali explained his thinking by saying: "Staying on the ropes is a beautiful thing for a heavyweight. When you stay on the ropes and make him shoot his best punches and he can't hurt you, you know you are going to win."

Foreman unsuccessfully chased Ali in the seventh, hoping to land a telling blow. But the steam of Foreman's punches had long since subsided, leaving him an exhausted punching bag for the taking. Late in the eighth round, Ali unloaded with a left-right combination that put Foreman on the deck. The champion remained on the canvas as Clayton counted him out.

"I guess when a fighter is knocked down, he doesn't see the punch," Foreman said. "A knockdown is something as a pro I

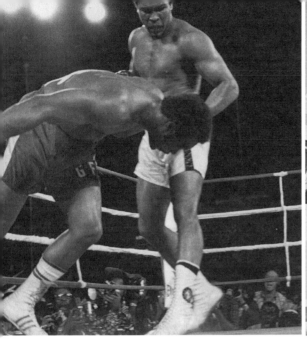

By the eighth round of their heavyweight title fight, Ali was fresh and Foreman exhausted. Ali had thrown fewer punches, but his were far more effective when it counted, including a left-right combination that sent his previously undefeated opponent to the canvas. Ali regained the championship more than seven years after it had been taken from him.

Ali, standing behind Illinois State Senator Charles Chew, returned to Chicago from Zaire celebrating the heavyweight championship he had regained with an eight-round knockout of Foreman. At age 32, Ali had won the title for the second time while improving his record to 45-2 with 31 knockouts. "The Greatest" was back on top.

never experienced. But then some great fighters have been down. I just didn't know the fight was over until I saw Ali's handlers in the ring."

Officially, Ali's knockout to regain the heavyweight championship came at 2:58 of Round 8. At the age of 32, after more than seven years had passed, Ali once again reigned as the champion. Floyd Patterson was the only other heavyweight to regain the title, after knocking out Ingemar Johansson in 1960 after Johansson had beaten him a year earlier. For Foreman, the loss was his first after 40 wins, which included 37 knockouts. For Ali, it pushed his record to 45-2 with 31 knockouts.

Shortly after Ali's combination ended the fight, he sat in the ring cutting the figure of someone who had not believed his own words. Once he left the ring, a heavy rainstorm emptied on the stadium and Ali again found his voice.

First he told reporters that his earlier comments about retirement were premature given the fact that he felt his title had been taken away from him unjustly. After winning it back, he wanted to hold on to it for a while. He also chastised oddsmakers, such as Jimmy "The Greek" Snyder, and the media.

"You made Foreman a saint," Ali said. "You made him the hard puncher. May you all regret your words and repent. That goes for Jimmy 'The Greek.' If you want to know anything about boxing, don't let anybody in Las Vegas tell you. Don't let the experts make an ass out of you."

Despite Foreman's disappointment in losing, he could see through Ali the promoter to Ali the person and the fighter.

"A true champion never complains, never bad-mouths an opponent," Foreman said. "I think Ali should be respected. He's a true American, a great gentleman, and he should be called the champion."

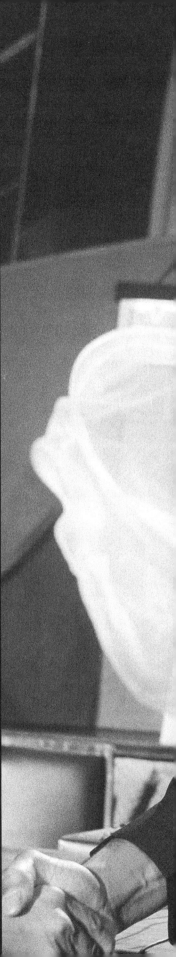

THRILLA IN MANILA

CHAPTER 14

At a July 17, 1975, news conference in New York, Ali told reporters that Joe Frazier would need a butterfly net to catch him in their October fight in Manila. The heavyweight champ also had a toy gorilla in his pocket. He compared Frazier to a gorilla during a ruthless verbal onslaught in the weeks preceding the fight.

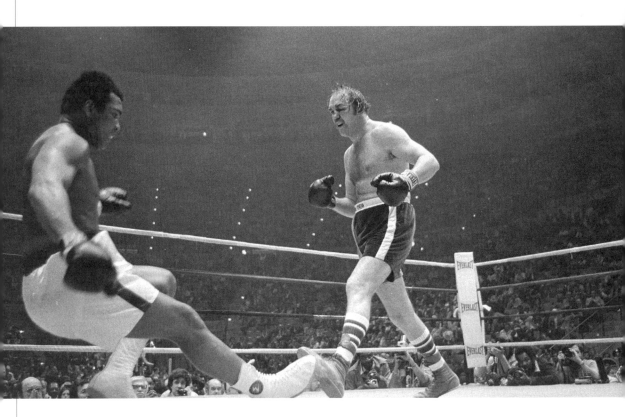

Thrilla in Manila

Though it was ruled a knockdown, Ali insisted he tripped over Chuck Wepner's foot during the ninth round of their 1975 heavyweight title match in Cleveland. Whatever the cause of the fall, it did not prevent Ali from returning to his feet and, in the 15th round, becoming the first man to defeat Wepner by knockout.

Muhammad Ali's win over George Foreman ushered in a new era in the heavyweight division—a period in which old warriors with diminishing skills displayed guile and unyielding heart. Lurking in the background for Ali was the inevitable finale with Joe Frazier.

While Ali prepared for his first title defense against Chuck Wepner, Frazier continued to remind fight fans that he was still a prominent contender. On March 2, 1975, Frazier improved his record to 32-2 with 27 knockouts when he sent Jimmy Ellis to the canvas in the ninth round.

Ali cherished the idea of again holding the heavyweight title, but he did not embrace the necessary training prior to the Wepner fight. Despite the fact that Ali had far superior boxing skills when compared to those of Wepner, the "Bulldog from Bayonne" was not a man to take lightly.

At age 34, the former liquor salesman from Bayonne, New Jersey, stood 6'5", held a record of 30-9, and had the reputation of being a brawler. Accompanied by former champion Floyd Patterson, Wepner visited Ali's camp in Deer Lake, Pennsylvania, two weeks before their March 24, 1975, fight. During the visit,

After 15 years in the professional fight game, Ali had lost much of his speed but remained as quick-tongued as ever. Prior to the Thrilla in Manila, he referred to Joe Frazier as "nothin' but a punchin' bag"…among other things.

Wepner told Ali: "You're as fat as a turkey and ripe for the plucking."

Ali, who had spent a career making brash statements about opponents, hardly blinked at Wepner's assessment. Talk promoted fights, and the reason Ali made large amounts of money for the bouts he fought was the interest he always generated. People cared what happened to Ali in the ring, and they paid their money accordingly to see the outcomes. So rather than get mad at Wepner's turkey comment, Ali simply went with the flow. Though he typically degraded the skills of boxers who could give him a true fight, Ali tended to build up those who really had no hope. Ali made Wepner sound like a threat.

"Fighting Muhammad Ali is Wepner's lifelong dream," Ali said. "He has no fear whatsoever…. Why, I've used all types of psyche…and he's still holding tight to the mike…. Wepner has the will. Muhammad has the skill. But if the will is greater than the skill, the will overpower the skill."

Ali also recognized his lack of conditioning, which showed. He sounded old and uninspired when he said he was "overtired and under-trained." He added, "It's a grinding, grueling job. There's no pleasure in the ring for me."

Ali wasn't the only one who commented on his subpar physique. At the weigh-in, hosted by ABC broadcaster Howard Cosell,

Ali tipped the scales at 223½ pounds, prompting Cosell to blurt: "Oh, my God?"

Nobody expected much from Wepner, so what they got in the way of a show proved interesting. Providing the periphery scenery that night in Cleveland was Frazier, who received some cheers but a disturbing chorale of boos as well. Frazier, who would not forget the hostile reception, blamed Ali. "Booed 'cause Clay had folks, black folks especially, believing that I was a traitor to my race," Frazier said.

Dick Young of the *New York Daily News* noted the distasteful texture of the incident when he wrote: "Black people boo Joe Frazier, unthinking black people, people who have let themselves be influenced by Muhammad Ali and his often crass exploitation of racism."

Anticipation for the Wepner fight was low, except for those who pulled for the "Great White Hope" with a slugger's chance. In the ninth round, Wepner did deliver a big blow. He hit Ali with a right to the ribs and sent him to the canvas, prompting the crowd of 14,847 to stand and cheer.

Ali claimed he tripped, and photographs showed that Wepner did step on his foot, contributing to the fall. After a mandatory eight count, Ali got to his feet and proceeded to finish off Wepner. The champ unleashed a series of blows in the 15th, handing Wepner the first-ever

Opposite left: Ali used the "rope-a-dope" and a tactic he termed the "mirage" against Ron Lyle. He protected his vital points while daring his opponent to spend all his energy throwing ineffective punches in the middle of the ring. He credited Lyle for fighting intelligently, but he was still able to stop his overmatched foe by TKO in the 11th round of their May 16, 1975, fight in Las Vegas.

Opposite right: Patrons at the 1975 International Book Fair in Frankfurt did not have to look far to find the author or the subject of a book entitled *The Greatest*. Ali was quick to give his own story a stamp of approval in the VIP room of the Frankfurt airport on his way to introducing the book to the masses.

Above: Frazier's remarks about Ali draw applause from Philippines President Ferdinand Marcos at the Malacanang Palace two weeks before the 1975 Ali-Frazier fight in Manila. Frazier had a personal score to settle with Ali, who had won their previous match and had been taunting "Smokin' Joe" mercilessly in the buildup to their third meeting. Marcos did not choose sides.

knockout of his career. Afterward, Ali took shots at referee Tony Perez.

"He's a dirty dog referee and let Wepner fight dirty," Ali said. "This was a disgrace to boxing. But I got out unmarked."

Ali moved on, readying for his fight with Ron Lyle, a 33-year-old ex-con who had been convicted of second-degree murder and paroled after serving seven years in a Colorado jail. Also on Ali's schedule was a fight with Joe Bugner, scheduled for June 30, 1975, at Merdeka Stadium in Kuala Lumpur.

Ali fought Lyle on May 16, 1975, in Las Vegas. Lyle had lost his previous fight to Jimmy Young, but it did not cause him to lose his title shot against Ali. Much like the fight against Wepner, Ali came off as a disinterested participant. Nevertheless, he came away the winner via a technical knockout in the 11th round.

Ali commended Lyle for fighting an intelligent bout and for figuring out that attacking the rope-a-dope was not the right tact. While addressing the media, he sounded like a lecturing professor.

"You may not realize what I have invented, but it is a new way of fighting," Ali said. "Every fighter is trained to get his man in a corner and go after him. By inventing the 'rope-a-dope,' I have made them psychologically afraid to go in after me. That already gives me a big edge because fighting me in the middle of the ring is fighting my way."

Because Lyle did not go after him in the corner, Ali went to a tactic he called the "mirage." He explained that the mirage was like the rope-a-dope only it was in the middle of the ring.

"He was smart enough not to chase me too much against the ropes, so I went to the mirage," Ali said. "I get out there, in punching range, with my hands up protecting the vital points, and he wears himself out punching at me."

Ali cited the risk involved with the rope-a-dope and the mirage, noting that a fighter could take a blow he might not be able to withstand while covering up. He surmised that he alone was the master of both techniques.

While he had the podium, Ali felt compelled to take another shot at Wepner, noting that his fight with him was tougher than his fight with Lyle because Wepner "was dirty and fought like a woman, and I was sore all over afterwards and I wasn't in as good shape. But Lyle fought much better."

Ali had not taken either Wepner or Lyle very seriously and had trained accordingly. But Bugner was different. For starters, Ali was familiar with Bugner from his earlier fight against him in February 1973, when it took him 12 rounds to claim a decision. In addition, Bugner was 25 and Ali was 33, a seasoned age for any fighter.

Ali sounded humble when talking about Bugner prior to the fight, and he took along former heavyweight champion Jimmy Ellis to serve as his sparring partner. Meanwhile, Bugner forecast that the heat in the outdoor stadium would be too much for Ali to withstand at his advanced age.

Yet it was Bugner who seemed to succumb to the heat. Bugner never got anything going, while Ali ran through his typical gamut of antics: dropping his hands, forcing the action at times, and shuffling. Ali took a 15-round decision that Dundee credited to his fighter's superior training.

"I tried," Bugner said. "I still feel confident that I will win the title, but I just didn't have it this time. I tried to use moving tactics for the first eight rounds and then step up the pace. Unfortunately, I just couldn't find the energy anywhere. I think the weather beat me. It's a good thing to move the championship fights around the world, but it's sometimes very unfair to the fighters."

With three minutes left in the fight, Ali called to Frazier and shouted: "You're next. Be ready!"

Afterward, Ali complimented Bugner. "I thought I would knock Joe out in 10 rounds, but I couldn't," he said. "Joe Frazier didn't give me such a rough time. Ken Norton didn't and George Foreman didn't."

Many experts did not consider Frazier a legitimate threat to beat Ali in their fight, which would be staged in Manila, Philippines. The Frazier bashers claimed that Ali had disposed of Joe rather easily in their 1974 rematch at Madison Square Garden. Some wondered why Ali even agreed to fight Frazier a third time, the answer to which stemmed from Ali's kindness. Yes, Ali regularly attacked his opponents' character, tendencies, style, or whatever he deemed fodder for promotion. But he also respected his opponents. Ali had respect for Frazier and felt that he wanted to give him an opportunity based on their history.

Dundee could not be counted among those belittling Frazier's chances against Ali. He felt Frazier was a dangerous opponent.

"Frazier on any given night could lick any given fighter because he was—he was for real," Dundee said.

Furthering Frazier's chances against his old adversary were the feelings of anger he held toward Ali. He had never forgiven him for the way Ali had depicted him as a "Tom" in their first fight, and he loathed the way Ali made fun of his looks, especially when he called Frazier "the gorilla."

Frazier believed that no fighter had given the way he had to boxing. "And yet the message that the bigmouth sent out was that I was a caveman with gloves, too stupid to get out of the way of the punches," Frazier wrote.

Ali kept his foot on Frazier's throat throughout the buildup to the fight. During a New York press conference held to promote the fight, Ali and his entourage burst in wearing black T-shirts with a picture of a gorilla on the front. Ali's tongue continued to rattle—and irritate—Frazier when he chortled: "It will be a killa and a chilla and a thrilla when I get the gorilla in Manila."

Ali wouldn't let it go. He kept a stuffed gorilla doll at his training camp and later touted a small, black rubber gorilla, all the while saying he was going to get the gorilla in Manila.

Ali's personal life also factored into the events leading up to the fight. He used his time away from the United States to be with Veronica Porche, a young woman he had grown smitten with the previous year in Africa. Ali's wife, Belinda, stayed at home with their kids while Ali carried on his affair with Porche in Manila.

Ali's personal agenda bore a stark contrast to that of Frazier, who had a personal score to settle with his longtime tormentor, Ali. The contrast brought a dangerous element to the fight—a danger that the Ali camp never seemed to sense.

A story in the *New York Post* ran a bunch of quotes the day before the fight, which seemed to reflect the lack of fear in Ali's camp. Ali was quoted as saying: "Joe Frazier is completely washed up. This is a pitiful fight. He ain't nothin' but a punchin' bag." Ali added: "Third round may be too long."

Even Dundee had changed his tune, making the observation: "This isn't the same

Opposite: Rather than using any of his tricks like the "rope-a-dope," Ali came out fighting aggressively against Frazier in Manila, going shoulder-to-shoulder with his nemesis. Ali won the first five rounds of the October 1, 1975, title bout at the Coliseum, seemingly determined to fulfill his own prediction and that of trainer Angelo Dundee that it would be a rout. His wily opponent had other ideas.

Ali managed to unload a sharp right to the head of Frazier in the ninth round, but it did not diminish Frazier's advantage in the middle rounds. Ali resorted to hooking a glove behind Frazier's head to buy time in those rounds, but Frazier pounded Ali's chin with hooks. The third meeting between the veteran heavyweights, the "Thrilla in Manila," became a battle of wills.

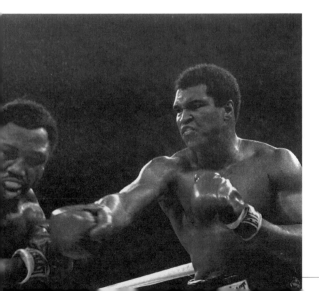

Joe Frazier. He's sluggish; his rhythm is off. Ali will kayo him. I guarantee it."

The fight took place on October 1, 1975, inside the Philippine Coliseum at 10:30 in the morning to coincide with a favorable viewing time in the United States. The building was air conditioned, but under the hot lights the temperature more closely resembled the sweltering climate outside the building.

Ali entered the ring wearing his customary white trunks with the black stripe and waistband. Frazier's gear was something out of the ordinary: baggy denim trunks. Ali immediately began to stare at Frazier, but his glare was more a continuation of the act. The stares returned by Frazier reflected more of a deep resentment.

Instead of relying on the "rope-a-dope" or the "mirage," Ali came out aggressively. From the outset, the Ali camp's predictions of a rout appeared on the money. Ali flicked combinations off Frazier's head throughout the first round, and twice during the round Frazier look woozy. Ali followed with another strong showing in the second round. However, the determined Frazier continued to move in on Ali, often leading with his seemingly indestructible head.

Though Ali took the first five rounds, his advantage gradually dwindled. By the fifth, those watching the fight understood that Frazier would not, as Dylan Thomas once penned, go gently into that good night. Ali began to sit back on the ropes, as he had successfully done in the Foreman fight and every fight since. Frazier understood the tactic and the risk of punching himself out, yet the chance to pummel away at his tormentor's ribs was too tempting for him. So he burrowed in close and cut loose with powerful body blows.

In the sixth round, Ali said to Frazier, "They told me you were through." Joe responded, "They lied, Champ, they lied."

"I think this is what dying is like."

—ALI, after the 10th round of the Frazier fight

Ali tried to slow down Frazier by resorting to an illegal yet rarely called tactic: hooking his glove around the back of the shorter Frazier's head and holding on. Eventually Ali did receive a warning by the referee, but it did not stop him from using the move. That was understandable since he wasn't employing a strategy but rather hanging on for dear life—like a man who can't swim clinging to a life preserver. Frazier still managed to land several devastating left hooks to Ali's chin.

Ali's corner grew concerned. As retold by Frazier, Dundee and Bundini Brown said, "Stop playing champ, Champ…. You got to float like a butterfly…. He'll call you Clay from now on. Make him call you Muhammad."

But no words could help Ali, who was absorbing a terrible punishment. At the conclusion of the 10th round, Ali slumped in his corner and told Brown, "I think this is what dying is like."

After losing the first five rounds, Frazier took the middle five. At this point, the training of each fighter came into focus. While Ali had trained and played, Frazier had gone the extra mile, training like a contender who understood that he would get just one shot at the title. Ali looked drained and out of steam heading into the 11th round. Frazier seemed full of pep and vigor.

Unfortunately for Frazier, Ali's punches earlier in the fight had been effective enough to cause swelling. Frazier already had limited vision in his left eye stemming from a cataract problem. So the swelling in his right eye became a critical factor, making it hard for him to see.

Ice bags were applied to Frazier's eyes with little effect on the swelling. If Frazier wanted to continue, he would have to fight on with little chance of seeing Ali's punches. He gamely continued.

Understanding his situation, Frazier unleashed everything he had in the 11th

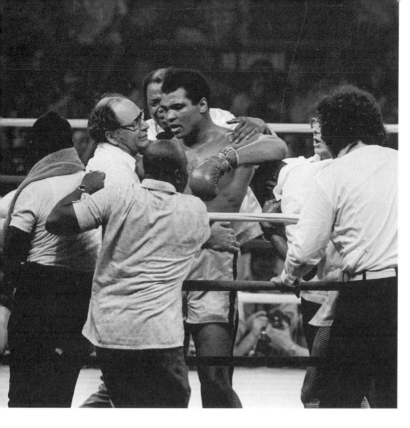

After 14 rounds of the "Thrilla in Manila," Joe Frazier could barely see out of his swollen eyes, and both fighters were spent. Ali, after being hit hard in the middle rounds, had been the aggressor in the 13th and 14th, and Frazier was unable to answer the bell for the final round. Ali's trainers, handlers, and doctors surrounded him after his 1975 victory in one of the most memorable bouts in history.

round, landing hooks and body punches with great regularity throughout the round. Dundee screamed at Ali to escape the corner, where Ali had camped on the ropes while Frazier continued the assault. Words did nothing to help Ali find the clear or slow down Frazier, yet when the bell clanged to end the round, Ali remained standing.

Frazier resumed his assault at the beginning of the 12th, but by the end of the round he looked like he finally was running on empty. Ali's corner called Frazier's condition to Ali's attention, and the champ found an unused reserve of energy. He went on the attack in the 13th and 14th rounds.

Suddenly the fight had evolved into something more than a championship fight. Two proud men were now battling to the death. The way each was fighting, it seemed, only one would remain standing at the end of the fight.

Ali sat in his corner following the 14th round and expressed his respect for Frazier

> "Lawdy, that man can take a punch!"
> —JOE FRAZIER, on Ali

when he said, "Lawdy, that man can take a punch!" Across the ring, trainer Eddie Futch asked his fighter, "What's with the right hand?" Frazier answered: "I can't see it. I can see the left, but when I move away, I get hit with the right."

Futch then did what he had to do by throwing in the towel, despite Frazier's protests. A roar went up from the crowd when Frazier did not answer the bell for the 15th. The disheartened Frazier sat slumped in his corner with Futch's hand resting on one shoulder, while a relieved Ali slipped down to the canvas on his back.

Afterward, Ali summoned Marvis Frazier to his dressing room. Frazier's young son obliged. He found the champ lying on a padded table, looking like the survivor of a car wreck. Ali sat up when Marvis came into the room and shook his hand.

"Tell your father all the stuff I said about him—I didn't mean it," Ali said. "Your father's a hell of a man. I couldn't have taken the punches he took tonight."

STILL THE KING

Fans around the Times Square theater where the biographical film *The Greatest* was playing on May 25, 1977, got a surprise visit from the subject of the movie. Ali made an unannounced stop outside the venue, mingling with fans and no doubt reminding them of the truth behind the movie's title.

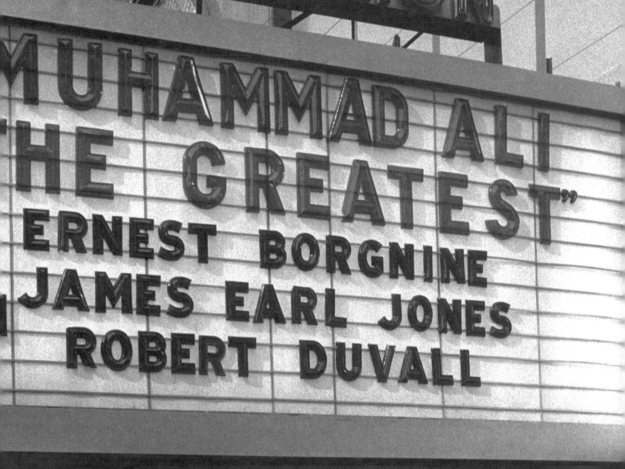

In his first true test since his "Thrilla in Manila" win over Joe Frazier one year earlier, Ali knew he trailed Ken Norton after 12 rounds of their September 28, 1976, fight at New York's Yankee Stadium. He decided at that stage to rack up points with his jab, which Ali did expertly over the final three rounds. The result was a split decision that preserved Ali's heavyweight championship but led to questions about whether he deserved the win.

STILL THE KING

STILL THE KING

Ali did not know at the time that he was having his own "brush with fame" when he embraced brothers Sedar (left) and Dave Chappelle in Silver Spring, Maryland, in 1976. Ali was in his hotel room before a fight with Jimmy Young, unaware that one of his young visitors—little Dave—would grow up to become a hugely popular comedian.

Muhammad Ali had survived a war against Joe Frazier in Manila in 1975, absorbing physical damage from which he never truly would recover. Many might have retired at that point, but not Ali. He enjoyed being the heavyweight champion, and he would continue to defend his title.

Ali took an extended hiatus following his brawl against Frazier. Physically, he needed to heal before stepping back into the ring. In less than top form, he finally returned to the ring five months after the Frazier fight on February 20, 1976, against lightly regarded Jean-Pierre Coopman.

A 29-year-old Belgian, Coopman had been fighting for just four years. He entered the bout with 27 professional fights under his belt, three of which he had lost. Though Coopman had won his previous 11 fights—seven via knockouts—he appeared to be the biggest "bum" that Ali had faced since the early 1960s. Wrote Robert Markus of the Chicago Tribune Press Service: "Ali has fought some stiffs before, but none with fewer credentials than the likeable Coopman...."

Ali could even be counted among those who liked Coopman. A day before the bout, he said, "He's such a nice guy, I can't get mad at him."

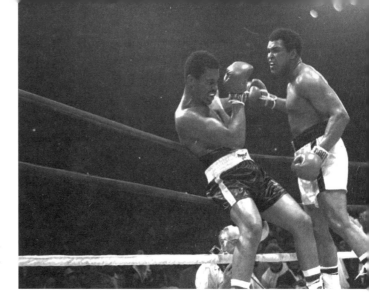

In just his second fight since his physically taxing victory over Joe Frazier in 1975, a 230-pound Ali proved too much for hungry challenger Jimmy Young in Landover, Maryland, on April 30, 1976. Though Ali later admitted he underestimated Young, his power and poise were enough to take a unanimous decision over 15 rounds. Many in the crowd, however, were disappointed in the effort.

Their encounter took place in front of 12,000 fans in the Roberto Clemente Coliseum in San Juan, Puerto Rico. Coopman allegedly drank champagne prior to the start of the fight, and Ali knocked him out in the fifth round.

Afterward, Ali admitted in so many words that he had fought a vastly inferior opponent. "He fell and I felt sorry for him," Ali said. "We live in a freakish world, a vicious world. People like to see blood.… People want life and death from me all the time.… Let me have a little rest in between."

Ali's next title defense came against Jimmy Young on April 30, 1976, in Landover, Maryland. Angelo Dundee classified Young as "a boxer, a cute fighter—not great, but a threat." Dundee worried about Ali staying motivated for the fight, and he reminded him about "San Diego" when Ali did not want to run one morning. Ali had not taken Ken Norton seriously prior to their bout in San Diego, and Ali ended up losing a 12-round decision and suffered a broken jaw.

Young, who trained in Joe Frazier's gym in Philadelphia, sounded hungry. "I never made more that $7,500 in a fight before this," Young said. "I don't even own a car. To me, this fight means the heavyweight championship, it means being on top, and most of all it means money. The cash—$85,000."

Despite entering the ring at a bloated 230 pounds, Ali prevailed in 15 rounds. Many of the 12,472 fans at the Capitol Centre booed the decision.

"I thought I won," Ali said. "But I would like to say that I underestimated Jimmy Young, that I didn't know Jimmy Young was so awkward, that he was as hard to hit, that he was as fast. I didn't worry about him. I took him lightly."

Not even a month later, on May 24, Ali returned to the ring to fight Richard Dunn in Munich, Germany. Ali had been embarrassed by how he had approached the Young fight and the resulting close decision, so he worked hard to get in shape for Dunn. As a result, he weighed in at 220 pounds, the lightest weight he had registered on the scale since regaining the championship from George Foreman two years earlier.

During the weigh-in for the fight, Ali dodged a potential disaster when the stage on which he and two dozen others were standing collapsed. Ali and the others fell through broken planks. Fortunately, nobody was seriously injured. Shortly thereafter, Ali began to speak his mind on a number of matters, his next opponent serving as one of the subjects. Ali, who did not regard Dunn as much of a threat, quipped: "What rhymes with Dunn? One!" As in a one-round knockout.

Ali looked forward to facing Norton, as if fighting him was a hurdle he needed to clear before getting to the place where he wanted

Yoko Ono and John Lennon joined Ali at the Inaugural Party in Washington, D.C., on January 19, 1977, the night before Jimmy Carter was sworn in as 39th president of the United States. Ali had been vocal in his support for Carter throughout the campaign.

to be. "I'm going to knock him out and then get out of the boxing business," Ali said. He also announced that after getting out of boxing he planned to fight a "wild animal in a cage with nothing but my bare hands."

During the period leading up to the Dunn fight, Ali exploded at different members of his entourage for their manner of indiscriminant charging over the years, which likely was a reflection of his finances. In a rage, he remarked to them: "I feed you niggers. I take you all over the world and you treat me like this. Nobody has this kind of crowd around him, not even Frank Sinatra."

Once in the ring, Ali at 220 pounds looked better than he had in most of his recent fights, and he knocked out Dunn in the fifth round. Afterward, Dunn smiled. "Ali gave me a tribute by being in shape," he said.

While Dunn wasn't the best litmus test for Ali's future, the fact that the champ took his opponent seriously and had worked himself into the necessary shape for the fight seemed to bode well for his upcoming bout with Norton, scheduled for September 28 at Yankee Stadium. In Ali's previous two fights with Norton, just one point on the judges' cards stood between the two fighters. Ali understood that after fighting a lot of less-than-qualified opponents, Norton represented the real deal. Their bout would be his first true test of boxing since the "Thrilla in Manila."

Ali had never badmouthed Norton prior to 1976, but he changed his tune this time around. Norton had appeared in the movie *Mandingo,* and Ali felt the role had perpetuated racial stereotypes. During a prefight medical exam, Ali called Norton, among other things, a "disgrace to your race" and a "yellow nigger."

Norton responded by addressing Ali's lifestyle. "I hate to get personal," Norton said. "But when he gets righteous about some of the roles I've played in films, let me remind you that those roles were fictitious. Why don't you check out his lifestyle? It's pretty real."

Norton added that he didn't mind Ali running his mouth, no matter what words came out. "All he's doing is selling tickets," Norton said. He added: "The promoters will want him to win. They believe they can make more money with him as champion. You might say I'm fighting Tuesday night against the whole boxing establishment. Let's face it: 75, 80 percent of the people are gonna be for Ali."

A canopy had not been constructed over the ring at Yankee Stadium, which led to speculation that the fight might be cancelled based on the constant rain and forecasts for more of the same. But the fight went on as scheduled, and a crowd of 30,298 gathered at the "House That Ruth Built."

Ali piddled around for most of the fight. At times this was due to Norton's awkward style; other times he went into his rope-a-dope. He danced a little and talked some smack. One thing was clear: After 12 rounds, Ali trailed Norton.

Recognizing this fact, Ali went to his jab to score points in the final three rounds. His efforts paid off with the judges, who awarded Ali a 15-round unanimous decision by scores of: 8-7, 8-7, 8-6-1. Norton appeared to be the most surprised person in Yankee Stadium. Once the decision was announced, tears welled up in his eyes. He took out his mouthpiece and began to taunt Ali.

"I know I won it, you know I won it," Norton said. "I think even Ali knows I won it. The fight speaks for itself. I outfought him completely. I wasn't even breathing hard. I've worked harder in the gym."

Whether it was reality or not, the perception left in the craws of those watching the fight was that the judges did not want to see the heavyweight champion lose his title via a decision. In the back of Ali's mind, he seemed to recognize the fact that the win might have been a gift.

"I can feel retirement around the corner," Ali said. "Age is catching up to me. I had just enough to win. I know I won. I think I pulled it out in the last round. That's what proves the champion from the trial horse."

Ali had made a great deal of money throughout his career, so retiring appeared an easy and viable option. But he also had lost a fortune to his ex-wives and entourage, leaving him just one option: keep fighting.

From a business perspective, Ali appeared to have a license to steal. He could schedule less-than-adequate opponents and continue cashing checks until the cows came home. That arrangement worked perfectly in his next title defense against Alfredo Evangelista.

Ali earned $2.75 million to fight against Evangelista on May 16, 1977, then won a 15-round decision over a far inferior opponent who showed no apparent boxing skills

> "I know I won it, you know I won it. I think even Ali knows I won it…. I outfought him completely."
>
> —KEN NORTON, after losing a controversial decision to Ali

The most famous boxer in the world met up with the actor who portrayed the most famous fictional fighter when Ali sparred playfully with Sylvester Stallone at the Academy Awards show in 1977. After Ali joked that Stallone had stolen his script, the two presented the award for best supporting actress. Stallone's *Rocky* won the coveted award for best picture.

whatsoever. Evangelista fit the profile of the fighters Ali needed to schedule. But his next opponent, Earnie Shavers, did not.

Dundee began to question whether Ali had reached his boxing mortality. "Maybe he's had it," Dundee said. "Ali is a champ, he's a clown, he is anything he has to be to make money. But after a while, it gets thin."

In Shavers, Ali faced one of the hardest punchers he had seen in his career. He wasn't anywhere near the boxing tactician that Ali was, but he wasn't in the ring to try and score a decision. He went for the bomb. Shavers resembled the baseball slugger who either hits a home run or air-conditions the building trying. The chances of the aging Ali not getting rocked by one of Shavers' bombs seemed plausible, which prompted the question of what the heck was Ali doing fighting Shavers.

The inevitable finally happened in the fourth round when Shavers attacked Ali, sending him back onto the ropes in a survival mode. Like a wounded animal seeking shelter, Ali managed to grab Shavers in a clinch. The move likely saved him from being knocked out in that round. Ali made it to the corner and was able to clear his head.

He had lived to fight another round. Through 14, Ali led the fight on points. Just before heading back into the ring for the final round, Ali remembered thinking, "Fight hard until you die."

The two fighters went toe-to-toe in the 15th round, with Shavers on the edge of ending the fight with any given blow. Only he didn't, and Ali took the decision.

"I'm tired," Ali said. "I'm so damn tired."

Ali had retained his title, but it appeared that his career had come to a close. Had he retired after the fight, he would have left with a 55-2 record, having redeemed his only losses (to Frazier and Norton) with two subsequent wins over each fighter. His record and legacy would have been virtually unblemished. But he chose to fight on.

"I'm tired. I'm so damn tired."

—ALI, after the Earnie Shavers fight

Ali took on one of the hardest punchers he had ever faced when he stepped into the ring against Earnie Shavers at Madison Square Garden on September 29, 1977. The imposing Shavers, shown here walking to a neutral corner after Ali slipped in the 14th round, nearly took Ali's title by knockout in the fourth round, but Ali held on and regained his senses. From then on, it was Ali's mission to rack up points and stay on his feet, a plan he pulled off to earn a unanimous decision.

JINXED BY SPINKS

CHAPTER 16

Ali turned to his "rope-a-dope" trick early in his February 15, 1978, title defense against Leon Spinks, covering up on the ropes while his younger opponent did all the punching. Ali underestimated the stamina of his younger opponent, who did not lose his edge in the later rounds as the champ had expected. Though 27 pounds lighter than Ali, Spinks delivered the harder punches for most of the bout.

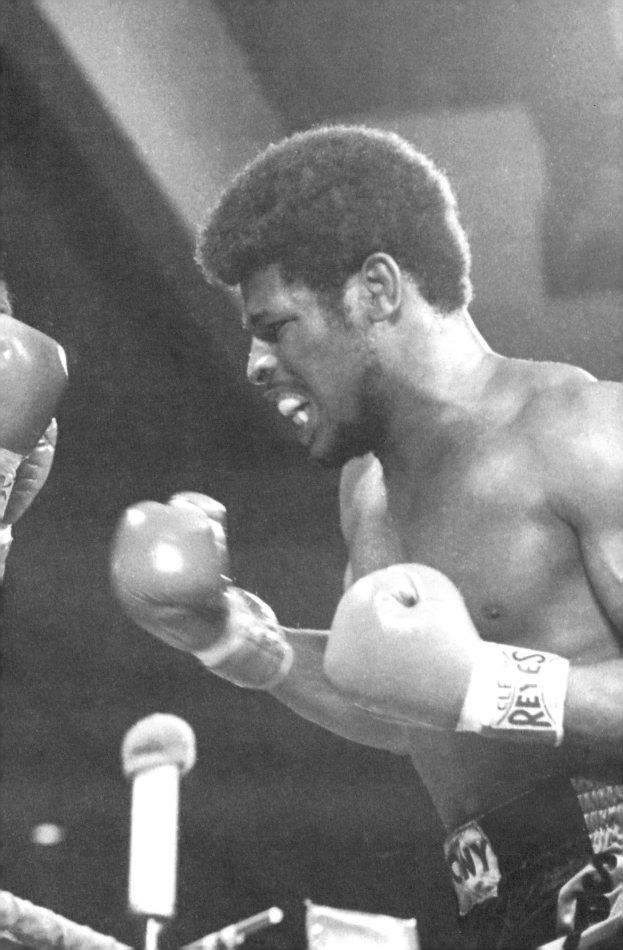

JINXED BY SPINKS

Leon Spinks *(right)* was young, hungry, and the owner of an Olympic gold medal when it was announced at this December 1977 news conference in New York that he would get a shot at the heavyweight title against Ali in February. Many felt that Spinks' brief pro career, 6-0-1 record, and erratic style did not seem to warrant such an opportunity against Ali, who had become uncharacteristically quiet in the weeks leading up to the fight.

Muhammad Ali needed to retire. That became obvious with each performance leading up to Leon Spinks. The question rang out: Why fight again?

Simple American capitalism brought the answer. Ali simply could not turn down the money.

Spinks grew up in poverty in St. Louis with six brothers and sisters. Frail as a youngster, Leon was directed to a boxing gym by his mother so he could learn how to take care of himself. By 1976 Leon, along with his brother Michael, had advanced to the top of the amateur ranks by earning spots on the United States Olympic team. Leon boxed as a light heavyweight and Michael as a middleweight. Both brought home gold medals.

Spinks was a former Marine corporal, but the discipline he achieved from military service did not translate to his boxing career. In addition to suspect training methods, he had technical problems in the ring. Few punches thrown in his direction missed because of his problems blocking them. And the punches he threw came from so far away that none registered as a surprise, leading them to be easily blocked. This was a bad combination.

Spinks registered knockouts in his first five professional outings before experiencing a 10-round draw in Las Vegas against Scott LeDoux, who had entered the match with a meager 21-6-1 record. Spinks then won a 10-round decision over Alfio Righetti of Italy on November 19, 1977. Despite his Olympic heroics, Spinks hardly had the credentials to earn a shot at the heavyweight title.

Ali's fight four and a half months earlier against Earnie Shavers had brought a ratings bonanza, which built up Ali's purse for a fight with Spinks. Whether Ali truly wanted to fight him or not may never be known, but he did opt to take the money. His purse for the fight was $3.5 million, while Spinks' share was $320,000.

Meanwhile, the press criticized Ali for fighting less than credible opponents. The attacks finally got to Ali, who decided in December 1977 that he would maintain silence during the time leading up to the fight. Thus, the most loquacious athlete in history was now mum.

Exemplifying Ali's uncharacteristic behavior was a news conference that he attended at Rockefeller Plaza, where he was supposed to promote a comic book that featured him knocking out Superman. Throughout the news conference, he clung to his policy of silence—even about the comic book. "I won't tell you nothin' about the book," Ali said. "I'm just tired of the press and I'm tired of people."

Bob Arum of Top Rank, which promoted the Ali-Spinks fight, defended Ali at the news conference. "He's 36 years old," Arum said. "He's troubled about something, and I think it may be because he's having a hell of a time training to get in shape at this stage of his career."

Ali had always been Spinks' hero when Leon was a youngster. But after watching the movie *Rocky,* Spinks embraced the underdog role. He even began to train in Joe Frazier's gym in Philadelphia, the hometown of character Rocky Balboa.

"I damn near threw my hat at the screen when he knocked the man down," said Spinks of Rocky. "Tears ran down my face."

Spinks was young and hungry at age 24. Ali was tired and bored at age 36. Spinks said of his pending fight with Ali: "I'm a peckin' chicken and Ali's got the gold that I really want."

Two days before he entered the ring to make his 12th title defense since beating George Foreman, Ali maintained his silence. So his trainer, Angelo Dundee, managed a few words, telling reporters that his fighter would knock out Spinks in the 11th or 12th round. He added: "But it'll be interesting early."

Dundee also spoke of the end for Ali. "You never know when the end of the rainbow ceases," he said. "You never know when he won't be able to do it." Dundee added that he didn't think even Ali knew when he wanted to retire. "But when he can't fight 100 percent and when he can't get up for a fight, when it becomes a complete bore to him, then he'll retire," Dundee said. "But not before that happens."

Ali went into the fight on February 15, 1978, as a heavy favorite and, according to Dundee, in the best shape he had been in since his first fight against Frazier. At the weigh-in, Ali tipped the scales at 224¼ pounds, 27 more than Spinks, which gave him the greatest weight advantage he had ever held over an opponent.

Ali finally talked on the afternoon of the weigh-in. Among other things, he ranted about how he was proud that he didn't have to talk if he didn't want to. He also said that Spinks was easy to hit with a right cross, and that the difference in age was the one thing that made the fight interesting. In the moments leading up to the fight, Jack Whitaker told a CBS audience that the only battle that would be seen this night was a ratings war between Ali and ABC's *Charlie's Angels.*

The Las Vegas Pavilion Hilton swelled with Ali fans yearning to see the aging champion put away Spinks. They quickly discovered that it wouldn't be the case. Spinks initiated the action in the early going. Ali went into his rope-a-dope defense, absorbing blow after blow of the Spinks onslaught. Later, Ali seemed content to dance and jab, confident that Spinks would run out of steam. Unfortunately for Ali, he miscalculated his challenger's determination and physical conditioning.

In the fifth round, Spinks landed a blow to Ali's lip that drew blood, but Muhammad did not appear to be in any real trouble. By the 10th round, Spinks finally looked tired, but he continued to rage on, employing a unique strategy. "Jab, jab, jab, that was the plan," said George Benton, Spinks' trainer. "Hit him on the left shoulder all night with that jab."

Somewhere in the midst of the fight, Ali remembered thinking: "This kid is a tough son of a bitch."

By the 14th round, both boxers understood that they were engaged in a close fight. This triggered a feverish slugfest between the two combatants, who did not want the judges to be the deciding factor. For both Ali and Spinks, a knockout would be the only way to ensure a win. Neither fighter could put the other away, and when the final bell rang, most felt that Spinks had fought well enough to win the bout. But had he won by enough of a margin to dethrone a champion?

Two of the ring officials had Spinks winning the fight, 145-140 and 144-141, while the third official gave the edge to Ali, 143-142. Since Nevada rules did not give the referee a vote, Spinks took the split decision.

Despite the loss, Ali still received support from the crowd when he left the arena. They cried, "Ali! Ali!" and "You're still the greatest!"

Afterward, Ali looked the part of the fighter who had hung around too long. The right side of his face was swollen. He knew he had lost the fight, and he was humble in defeat. "If I had to lose the title, I'm glad that I lost to a real man," he told reporters. He added: "Spinks proved all of you wrong. All you people didn't think he'd win."

Ali, shown greeting a young fan outside his Pennsylvania training complex, had become more quiet and introspective in his mid-30s. In fact, trainer Angelo Dundee may have done more talking than his fighter entering Ali's first bout with Spinks in 1978. Many began wondering whether Ali had reached the end of his road as a dominant fighter.

Some expected Ali to announce his retirement after the fight. He did not. Instead, he spoke about winning the title for a third time. "I'll be the first one to get it for the third time," he said. "I'll get in better shape. I'll get down to about 215 next time. I made a mistake in the early rounds. I was hoping he'd tire. He didn't tire."

Spinks did not promise Ali a rematch, but Ali knew he would get one because the public would demand one. And, he said, "The only one who can make him a few million in one night is me."

Spinks beamed afterward. "I'm proud of myself," he said. "I trained hard and I wanted to win. For the next few months, I want to relax."

And relax Spinks did during the months leading up to the September 15, 1978, rematch in the New Orleans Superdome. During that period, Spinks—who many had believed was an earnest ex-Marine—showed his true colors. Approximately a month after pulling off the upset, St. Louis

> "This kid is a tough son of a bitch."
>
> —ALI, on Spinks

police arrested Spinks for driving the wrong way on a one-way street. He did not have a driver's license and was in possession of a small amount of cocaine.

Spinks ran through all of his money on a variety of vices, and he did not train as he had for the first fight. Arum, who again promoted the fight, constantly had to battle to keep Spinks away from the French Quarter.

Ali cut a different figure than the dour, aging champion he appeared to be before his first fight with Spinks. He seemed rejuvenated as the challenger, and he trained hard. "All my life I knew the day would come when I'd have to kill myself," said Ali about his training. "To win, all I need to do is suffer. I don't want to lose and spend the rest of my life saying, 'Damn, I should have trained harder.'"

And once again, Ali was running his mouth in staccato fashion. "When I beat Sonny Liston, I shocked the world," he said. "When I joined the Muslims, I shocked the

Leon Spinks, age 24, celebrated after wresting the heavyweight championship from Ali in a stunning upset in Las Vegas on February 15, 1978. The former Olympic champion took a split decision as an 8-1 underdog, thanks to several convincing early rounds and an inspired finish. After the fight, fans cheered for Ali, assuring him that he was still "The Greatest."

Ali trained hard for his rematch with Spinks and used none of his old tricks during the September 15, 1978, bout at the Louisiana Superdome in New Orleans. He drilled Spinks with combinations and used his sharp jab and slick footwork to frustrate the newly crowned champ. The crowd responded with chants of "Ali! Ali!"

Opposite: In convincing fashion, Ali fulfilled his prefight vow to become the first man in history to win the heavyweight championship three times. His jabs and combinations were too much for the less skilled and less determined Spinks in their rematch. Ali won the 15-round fight by unanimous decision.

world. When I beat George Foreman, I shocked the world. I am from the House of Shock." He added: "You can't write a movie no better than this."

A crowd of 63,532 flocked to the Superdome for Ali-Spinks II expecting to see Ali redeem himself. Though no longer the champion, Ali remained the favorite, with the odds set at 12-5.

This time, Ali did not resort to rope-a-dope tactics or any other kinds of ring gimmicks. Using a stinging jab throughout the fight, he showed the footwork of a younger man while positioning himself to pepper Spinks with potent combinations.

In contrast, Spinks looked confused. Not helping matters was the rabble of unqualified handlers in his corner, who offered too much advice. Benton, the one man who should have been in Spinks' corner, grew so

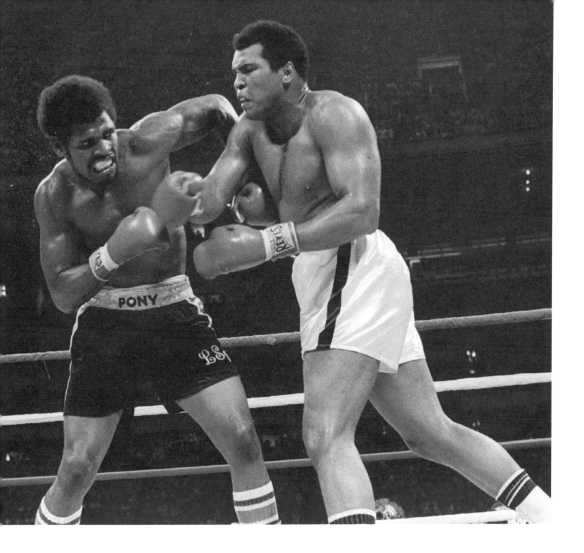

frustrated with the situation that he left the arena in the fifth round. Several times during the contest, fights broke out among Leon's handlers.

Ali had the fight well under control by the middle rounds, and he even showed off his famed Ali shuffle in the 10th round. The lopsided nature of the fight prompted Spinks to try to land one big blow. But every time he tried to do so, Ali slipped the punch and countered with stinging blows. In the late rounds, chants of "Ali! Ali!" reached a crescendo that rang throughout the Superdome—and didn't end until the final bell.

In a verdict that was unchallenged, Ali was awarded a 15-round unanimous decision.

He dethroned Spinks while thrusting himself once again to a position atop the boxing world.

"My mind wasn't on the fight," Spinks said. "Who knows what I was concentrating on; it certainly wasn't the fight.… I didn't feel like I felt the first time. It wasn't in my heart, maybe because a lot of things were on my mind, a lot of things the heavyweight championship brought me, a lot of problems."

Afterward, Dundee called the fight a "beautifully sloppy" bout. Vindicated, Ali hinted that he had fought his last fight. It would have been a fairytale ending for history's most beloved boxer. But unfortunately, Ali wasn't ready to bid farewell.

ALI'S
FINAL ROUNDS

CHAPTER 17

Ali came out light on his feet and called Larry Holmes "every name in the book and some out of the book" during their October 1980 fight in Las Vegas. But though he was only a 3-1 underdog, the 38-year-old Ali was no match for the undefeated heavyweight champion. Holmes pounded his former mentor in workmanlike manner, winning every round until Ali could not answer the bell for the 11th.

Two years after announcing his retirement, a 38-year-old Ali was back at it, heckling heavyweight champion Larry Holmes at a 1980 news conference in New York while hyping their upcoming fight. The unbeaten Holmes was a former sparring partner and a regular at Ali's Pennsylvania training complex, but that did not stop the former champ from calling him "the peanut" and promising to "shell" him.

ALI'S FINAL ROUND

Ali landed more verbal jabs than he did physical ones during his loss by TKO to former sparring partner Holmes in Las Vegas in 1980. "Is that all you got?" the three-time champion would ask the reigning champ, despite the fact that Ali was absorbing punch after punch while never mounting a serious attack of his own. Holmes looked several times at the referee, wondering when the fight might be halted.

There was no reason to think that Muhammad Ali was lying. He had spoken passionately about it throughout his career, and for two decades the media disseminated that information to the masses. Ali always maintained that he would not fight as an older man. Peering at boxing history through the eyes of an indomitable hero, he often looked back with pity at the lives of Joe Louis and Sugar Ray Robinson—two of his idols—and promised he would not make the same mistake.

Yet at 38 years old, Ali was about to climb back into the ring. And while 38 is hardly old, it's old for a fighter—particularly one who was about to challenge the best heavyweight in the world.

Ali officially announced his retirement in 1978 after defeating Leon Spinks to regain the heavyweight title an unprecedented third time. His legacy was secure. He even told a Long Beach, California, newspaper, "I'd be the biggest fool in the world to go out a loser after being the first three-time champ. None of the black athletes before me ever got out when they were on top. My people need one black man to come out on top. I've got to be the first."

Yet two years later, he was returning to the ring to fight a former sparring partner who also happened to be the unbeaten heavyweight champion of the world—Larry Holmes.

Trainer Angelo Dundee *(left center)* and cornerman Bundini Brown looked on with concern as Ali, the fighter they watched dominate the heavyweight division, absorbed a licking at the hands of Holmes in the 10th round of their 1980 fight in Las Vegas. Dundee had seen enough. He did not allow his fighter to get off the stool for another round, giving Holmes the victory by TKO.

There were already concerns about Ali's health and the ramifications of what more punishment might reap later in his life. Beginning in 1977, Dr. Ferdie Pacheco—Ali's longtime cornerman and personal physician—refused to work with the champ because of a report that the fighter was already suffering kidney damage. But the Mayo Clinic and the Nevada State Athletic Commission deemed Ali fit to fight.

If the bout was a mistake for a Ali, it was a no-win situation for Holmes. "If I won, everyone would just say I beat an old man," Holmes said. "If I lost, they'd say, well, he never could fight. He didn't have the heart."

It would be Holmes' heart that would pose the biggest obstacle to his success. He was still emotionally attached to Ali. At a time when the boxing community saw little value in the raw, unpolished heavyweight that was Holmes, Ali personally escorted him behind the scenes for a glimpse at the biggest show in sports. Holmes was a regular at Ali's Deer Lake training camp, and he later traveled the world as his chief sparring partner. The first time that Ali gave him a black eye, a camp aide offered Holmes a bag of ice for the swelling. He refused it, saying, "No, I'm going to drive all the way back to

"People like to be mystified; that's why they believe in ghosts and miracles. I predict a miracle." —ALI, on his upcoming bout against Larry Holmes

Easton [Pennsylvania] to show everyone the black eye Muhammad Ali gave me."

That kind of pride and respect was hard to dismiss, even for a $2.3 million purse.

"Ali gave me a job," Holmes said. "I didn't have any money, but he gave me $500 a week. He took me around the country, around the world. And you learned just by watching him. I sat in the back and watched everything he did. When he was in the ring, I was in the back, watching."

It could be argued that during that time, he also learned how to beat Ali. But that was a notion that "The Greatest" would not consider feasible. If there is one common trait among all great fighters, it is the unwavering belief in their ability. The great ones believe they are invincible.

Of course, that was something Ali had to sell to the public. And there was no better pitch man than Muhammad. "Sometimes your mind can make your body do things it shouldn't be able to do," he told the media. "I like to prove people wrong. People like to be mystified; that's why they believe in ghosts and miracles. I predict a miracle."

Throughout his career, Ali had given his opponents nicknames. Sonny Liston was the big, ugly bear; Floyd Patterson was the rabbit; and Joe Frazier was the gorilla. Suddenly, Holmes became the peanut because of the shape of his head. Ali playfully promised to "shell" him during the fight.

But as the fight drew closer, the prefight verbiage turned to venom. "Larry's living under an illusion he beat me every day in the gym," Ali said. "Holmes would not be around if Joe Frazier was in his prime. Holmes would not be around if George Foreman was in his prime…. This man's not as good as Leon Spinks. He's not as fast. He's straight up. Spinks, he ducks and crouches…. He's nothing. He's just the man between me and my fourth title."

As the fight drew near, Ali's persona began to sway the public. With Ali a 3-1 underdog, gamblers started laying money on the former champ, and the media began buying his rhetoric. Maybe it was habit, or maybe they just didn't want to believe that the greatest fighter of their generation was no longer that.

Steve Farhood, a boxing broadcaster for Showtime, was the editor-in-chief of *KO Magazine* at the time. He recalled how easy it could be to be swayed by the great Ali. "Given what we all knew, I remember thinking that the odds were absurd," he said. "But I wouldn't bet the fight. I think the Ali mystique was so great that you kind of expected some magic. With Ali, it was easy to suspend the truth."

"It was unbelievable," recalled Richie Giachetti, Holmes' trainer. "These were so-called boxing experts in the media picking Ali to win. But Ali had slipped. Larry had no fear of him because they sparred so much. I saw Larry spar 1,000 rounds with Ali. And Larry got the better of him. Things weren't going to be different in a real fight."

"None of the black athletes before me ever got out when they were on top. My people need one black man to come out on top. I've got to be the first." —ALI

The bout took place on October 2, 1980, at Caesars Palace in Las Vegas. Holmes, 30 years old, weighed 211 pounds. Ali, eight years his senior, weighed 217. He was trim and sculpted. It was the lowest he weighed for a fight since 1974 when he upset George Foreman.

It was time for Ali to "shock the world" again. It's what he did best. Ali carried his familiar bravado into the ring, executing his famous staredown during the prefight instructions. In those tense, soul-searching moments before the bell, he was the picture of confidence. It was right there that many a fighter would be psychologically defeated by the Ali mystique. Ali bounced on his toes with the purpose and agility of a younger man. He certainly looked the part. But sadly, he could no longer pull off the role.

It was hardly a fight. Holmes asserted his superiority with the first jab he landed, and he reluctantly inflicted a methodical beating upon Ali. In reality, he was fighting himself far more than he was fighting Ali.

"I didn't want to," Holmes said. "But I had to. Ali knew I was a good fighter from all those years we sparred. He respected me, but he was still going to try and take my head off."

It was clear by the third round that Ali had nothing left. All he did was talk to Holmes. "He called me every name in the book and some out of the book," Holmes said. "I was shocked. This was Muhammad Ali. He'd say, 'You can't beat me, you can't beat your master.' I would hit him as hard as I could in the kidney, and he'd say, 'Is that all you got?'"

The fight, scheduled for 15, lasted 10 ugly rounds before Angelo Dundee stopped it with Ali sitting on his stool. Muhammad never went down, but he never mounted a serious threat. At times, Holmes would pause and glance at the referee, hoping he would stop the slaughter. Ali lost every single round, an indignity rarely suffered by boxing royalty.

"It was pathetic to watch," Farhood said. "You knew the only reason Holmes was hitting Ali was because he had to. And the only reason Ali was still there was because he had a tremendous heart."

It was clearly over. Everyone seemed to know and accept this but the man himself. Ali had spent his career defying the odds, using his intelligence as much as his physical gifts to dominate boxing the way no one ever had before. But he could not see—or, more precisely, refused to see—that stepping into the ring again was a serious risk to his well-being. Always the sharpest guy in the room, Ali ignored what was obvious to the rest of the world after the Holmes fight.

He decided to fight on.

Ali spent four days in the hospital after absorbing the terrible beating from Holmes. There was a controversy over thyroid medication that Ali may have taken to lose

> "Father time caught up with me. I'm finished."
>
> —ALI, calling it quits after the Trevor Berbick fight

weight during the buildup to the Holmes fight. That ultimately provided a built-in excuse for his return to the ring. The sell to the boxing public this time was that it was the medication, and not Larry Holmes, that got the better of Ali.

"I wasn't surprised that he came back," Farhood said. "After the Holmes fight, you kind of had the feeling he wanted to go out better. I learned quickly that retirement is not a word you take literal in boxing."

Trevor Berbick, like Holmes, entered his fight against Ali with questions few fighters ever face.

"It was a great motivation to fight him," said Berbick. "But then there was a sympathy. I'm saying, how can I ever really, really hurt him, try to really hurt him seriously? I was hoping that I'd hit him and he'd just go down and out instead of banging at him hard. I knew I had to do what I had to do. So I stayed with the body because I figured it would do less damage."

If the Holmes bout served as a funeral for the Ali mystique, the Berbick fight was the burial.

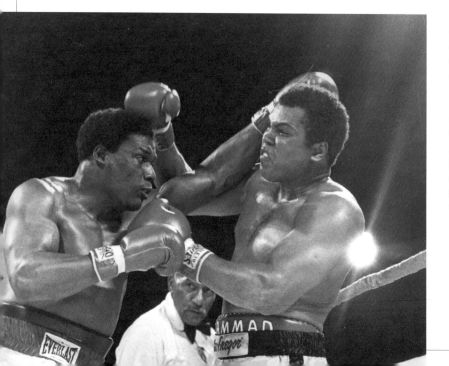

Because no American state would sanction another fight for Ali, he traveled to the Bahamas to tangle with Canadian Trevor Berbick in December 1981. Just one month away from his 40th birthday and at his heaviest fighting weight of 236 pounds, Ali was not even a shadow of his former self. Ali's goal was to go out in style, but instead he suffered a loss by unanimous decision.

The fight took place on December 11, 1981, in a baseball stadium in the Bahamas. The remote locale was chosen not because of the serene beaches and bright sun. Rather, the fight ended up there because not a single state in America would host it.

Berbick, 27, had already lost a title fight to Holmes but was still considered a Top 10 contender. He eventually would go on to win the WBC version of the heavyweight title, but that would come during an era when the heavyweight ranks were barren of talent. Berbick was a slightly better than average fighter. He possessed an awkward style and a clubbing-like power in his punches.

Ali was a month shy of his 40th birthday and weighed a career-high 236 pounds, 18 more than Berbick. The fight was dull, and even though one judge gave Ali three rounds, Berbick scored a unanimous 10-round decision.

"Father time caught up with me," Ali said after the fight. "I'm finished. I know it's the end. No excuses this time, but at least I didn't go down. No pictures of me falling through the ropes."

It was interesting that Ali chose those words. In the final fight of his career, Joe Louis was humiliated by a young Rocky Marciano, getting knocked through the ropes and counted out at Madison Square Garden.

Muhammad Ali would never fight again. The greatest career in heavyweight boxing history had come to an end. And for one final time, he and Joe Louis would share a common, inglorious bond.

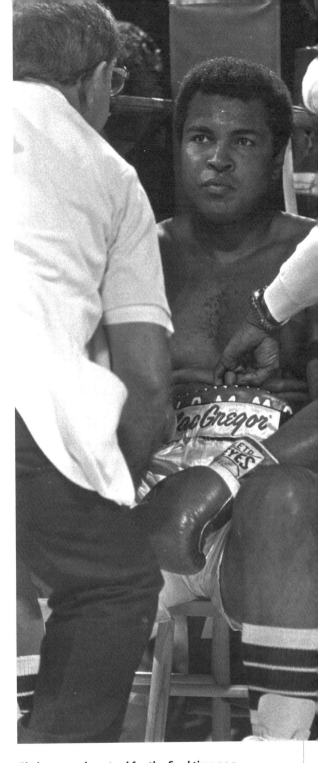

Sitting on a ring stool for the final time as a boxer, Ali prepares for the 10th round of his 1981 loss to Berbick. It was not the way his fans wanted to remember the man who once owned the heavyweight division while becoming the first man to win its championship three times.

THE GREATEST

CHAPTER 18

Ali threw himself into social
causes after leaving the ring
for good. He had a kiss for
a Liberian orphan upon his
arrival at an orphanage for
Liberian refugees in San Pedro,
Ivory Coast, in 1997. He and his
handlers were there to donate
food, wheelchairs, and medicine to about 400 orphans
after receiving a letter asking
for help from the mission's
organizer.

THE GREATEST

President Bill Clinton shows his appreciation for Ali during an awards ceremony at the 25th Anniversary National Italian American Foundation in 2000. Ali and trainer Angelo Dundee came to Washington, D.C., to receive the NIAF One America Award. It was just one of many service awards that have been bestowed on Ali in his post-boxing years.

It has been said that Muhammad Ali has been photographed more than any other person in history. Even if there is a president, supermodel, or dictator that could challenge Ali in this category, no one can doubt that he has been centered in a photographer's frame more than any other *athlete* who has ever lived.

Thus, there are enduring images of Ali, brought to life by chemicals in a darkroom and frozen forever in the imagination of a nation.

Remember…

Ali standing over Sonny Liston in 1965, shouting for the former champion to rise from the canvas. Or Ali on his back courtesy of a Joe Frazier left hook in 1971 at Madison Square Garden, boxing shoes aloft, tassels dancing in the smoky ringside air. Then there is a defiant Ali looking downward in Zaire in 1974, as George Foreman twists slowly to the canvas.

And, of course, there is the man away from the ring, the pop celebrity, hamming it up with the Beatles at the Fifth Street Gym in 1964. Or the black nationalist, striding alongside Malcolm X through the streets of Harlem in 1963.

There are two sets of images because there are two Alis, the athlete and the activist. Each has a separate legacy, and each is

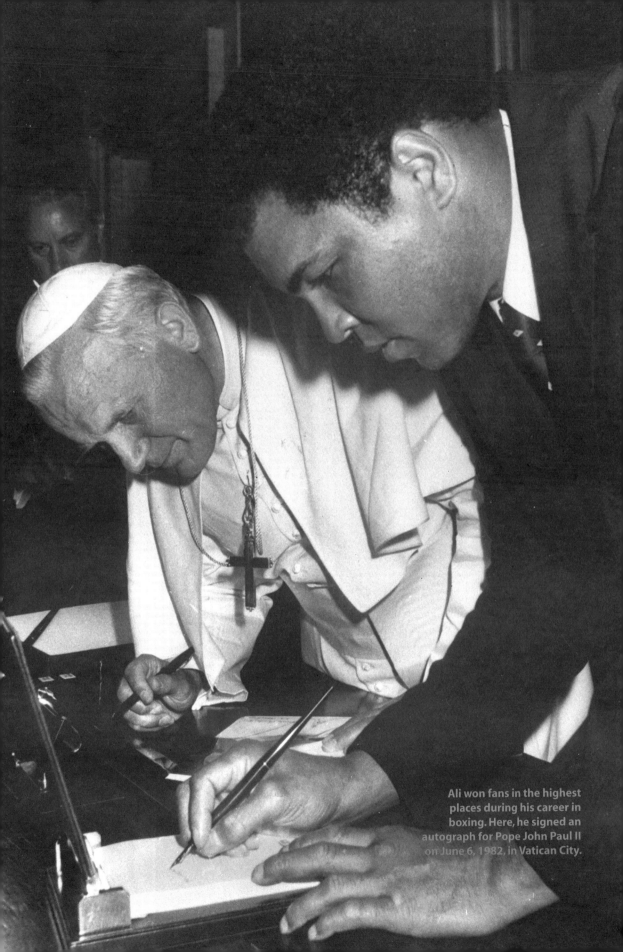

Ali won fans in the highest places during his career in boxing. Here, he signed an autograph for Pope John Paul II on June 6, 1982, in Vatican City.

In a moment that touched the world, Ali lit the torch for the 1996 Summer Olympics in Atlanta. It had been 26 years since he had won Olympic gold himself in Rome as Cassius Clay.

Actor Michael J. Fox jokes with Ali before the start of a 2002 Senate subcommittee on Labor, Health, Human Services and Education hearing on Parkinson's disease in Washington, D.C. Each battling Parkinson's, the celebrities were asking the panel for more funds for Parkinson's research.

"I think when Ali was at his best, he would have beaten any heavyweight champ in history."

—GEORGE CHUVALO

undeniably important. Ali branded his generation with courage and conviction in and out of the ring.

Within the realm of his sport, Ali was not just a fighter; he was a showman. He was a tireless promoter of his fights. When Ali was involved, boxing became entertainment. If fighters from previous generations were monosyllabic, Ali was a run-on sentence. While other fighters delivered cliché-ridden quotes to the media, Ali filled reporters' notebooks with predictions, poetry, and thought-provoking prose. He was accessible, candid, and often controversial.

But Ali also redefined the rules of how men fought. He ignored standard techniques that had been in practice since men began throwing punches at one another inside a ring. He abandoned all the rules of defense, yet early in his career he was incredibly hard to hit. He often threw punches without a firm foundation beneath him, yet he still could jolt an opponent. His hand speed was unparalleled in the heavyweight division. And his ability to absorb a punch ranks with the best in history.

The techniques that Ali introduced to boxing in 1960 are now seen in rings all over the world, from four-round pugs to world champions. His style has been emulated more than that of any other fighter.

What made Ali a great fighter was his competitiveness. He was at his best at the most trying moments. When the ring was spinning and the crowd a blur and the punches bursting like tiny bomb blasts on the battlefield that was his body, Ali thrived. He bit down hard on his mouthpiece and returned the punches even harder. If an opponent was lucky enough to survive Ali's considerable skill, then he was ultimately undone by Muhammad's indomitable will.

Ali was the first man to win the heavyweight title three times, and in achieving that feat he cleaned out two generations of fighters. When he turned pro in 1960, the heavyweight division consisted of a talented lot of fighters, and future Hall of Famers Sonny Liston and Floyd Patterson were at the head of the class. Ali easily defeated each man, twice. But when Ali returned from exile, the heavyweight division was at an all-time peak. Many boxing observers consider the early and mid-1970s as the greatest era in heavyweight history. Along with Ali, fellow champions Joe Frazier, Ken Norton, and George Foreman have been inducted into the International Boxing Hall of Fame. It has been suggested that many of the contenders of that time— Jerry Quarry, George Chuvalo, Ron Lyle, and Earnie Shavers—could have been champions in almost any other era. Ali beat all of them.

In 1998 *The Ring* magazine, long considered the bible of boxing, rated Ali the No. 1 heavyweight in boxing history. In 1999 Ali was crowned "Sportsman of the Century" by *Sports Illustrated* and the BBC.

Chuvalo was one of two men (Patterson is the other) to have fought Ali before and after the exile. "I think when Ali was at his best, he would have beaten any heavyweight champ in history," Chuvalo said. "People talk about Joe Louis. Well, Louis had trouble with Billy Conn, who was a smaller version of Ali. It's easy for me to say this because it was my era, but I really believe that Ali fought in the best heavyweight era in history. And Ali didn't turn his back on too many opponents. You just had to get in line."

Another former opponent, Chuck Wepner, agrees with Chuvalo. "I'd have to put Ali right near the top of the list," he said. "Ali, Louis, and [Rocky] Marciano are the three best heavyweights in history. In his prime, with his speed and power, Ali was tough to beat. He faced a lot of good heavyweights. When Rocky was champ, there weren't as many good heavyweights. And Louis had his 'Bum of the Month Club.'"

Eddie Futch, the Hall of Fame trainer, often sparred with Louis when both men were teenagers in Detroit. He would later devise the strategy for Frazier and Norton to defeat Ali. "I think Louis was the best heavyweight champion in history," he said. "Ali is second. Louis would have had a tough time with Ali's speed and boxing ability. Billy Conn demonstrated that. Conn was one of the most skillful boxers of his day. But Louis would eventually catch up with Ali like he did with Conn. Louis boxed Primo Carnera, Abe Simon, and Buddy Baer, so size didn't matter as much. Louis had lightning-quick hands, and all his punches were thrown correctly."

Ali, much like John F. Kennedy, Martin Luther King, and Robert F. Kennedy, represented a changing of the guard in the turbulent 1960s. It was a time when people believed they could make a difference, and Ali embodied that spirit. He was an outspoken critic of racial injustice, and his words stung a divided nation—angering some and inspiring others.

"As is the case with most great men, Ali was a product of his time," said Steve Farhood, a commentator for Showtime and a boxing historian. "It's almost impossible to imagine such a socially and politically impactful athlete today. Remember the infamous quote from Michael Jordan, who years ago was asked to endorse a Democratic candidate in North Carolina? He said, 'Republicans buy sneakers, too.' With that said, Ali was also well ahead of his time, a black man who was willing to emphasize his color at a time when it was not only controversial, but risky, to do so."

Farhood continued: "Until Ali, athletes were thought to be little more than dumb jocks who contributed only in the arena or on the playing field. Ali wasn't dumb, nor was he a jock. Over the course of a unique career, but especially in the '60s and early '70s, he redefined what greatness could mean."

Ultimately, Ali's stand against the Vietnam War made a greater impact on American society than his boxing career did. He was a hero to the antiwar movement and to the nation's growing counterculture. But in a broader sense, his steadfast commitment to his beliefs, despite the consequences, endured longer than his title fights. Many of those who found him deplorable in the moment wound up appreciating the man, and not just the fighter, with the passage of time.

"The thinking of the world was different in the '60s," said Dave Anderson, the Pulitzer Prize-winning sports columnist for *The New York Times*. "You can't ask people to write or think in a different time period. People disliked him for a variety of reasons. The racists hated him because he was black. Religious people hated him because he was a Muslim. And a lot of people disliked him just because he was a braggart. Then you had the Army thing on top of it. But [the media] grew to love him. He was always available. Early on he was more confrontational, but he was available. Some of the Muslims would say, 'You can't talk to him.' But then Ali would say, 'Yes, you can.' He was the best when it came to dealing with the media. He made it fun. The fighters before him were quiet guys. With Ali, there was this great breath of fresh air."

> "He made it fun. The fighters before him were quiet guys. With Ali, there was this great breath of fresh air."
>
> —DAVE ANDERSON, *New York Times* columnist

Ali continued to be part of history, even though his fighting days were long gone.

If one had to select a photo symbolic of Ali today, it would be his lighting of the Olympic torch at the 1996 Olympic Games in Atlanta. The torch relay in 1996 was a celebration of great American athletes, past and present, which included heavyweight champion Evander Holyfield. The final leg was carried by Olympic swimmer Janet Evans. As she ascended a ramp, Ali emerged from the background. Evans then lit Ali's torch, which he raised to the crowd's approval with his right hand. His left hand shook uncontrollably, due to his battle with Parkinson's syndrome. He then grasped his torch with two hands and lit the Olympic flame, signifying the official start of the games.

The image of Ali that night was a troubling reminder of what the champion had become and what peril can lie ahead for a fighter. Parkinson's syndrome is a nonfatal neurological disorder that often develops in patients over 60. Ali was first diagnosed at the age of 42, and its onset was due to an extended career in the ring. The characteristics that Ali displays—tremors, poor balance, and difficulty speaking—are all a byproduct of Parkinson's. Among the causes for people who are diagnosed at a younger age is repeated physical trauma. In the case of Ali, that physical trauma was a result of fighting. While his symptoms affect his motor skills and speech, Ali has not been incapacitated intellectually. His thought process has been unaffected, and his memory is said to be very good.

One of Ali's daughters, Laila Ali, also rose to prominence through boxing. Although Muhammad was reluctant to endorse women's boxing, he fully supports his daughter's career. She became a world champion and, in the biggest fight of her

career, won a majority decision over Jackie Frazier-Lyde, the daughter of Joe Frazier. It was billed as Ali-Frazier IV and was the centerpiece event of the 2001 International Boxing Hall of Fame induction weekend.

"Muhammad Ali is the most well known athlete in history," said Edward Brophy, executive director of the International Boxing Hall of Fame. "His charisma still transcends the sport of boxing." Ali has been the subject of an Academy Award-winning documentary, *When We Were Kings,* and the motion picture *Ali,* which earned actor Will Smith an Oscar nomination for his portrayal of Muhammad.

Even today, Ali is not confined to the world of sports and entertainment. He has served as a "messenger of peace," visiting Afghanistan and Iraq to help broker peace and foster understanding between Western and Islamic cultures. In 2005 the Muhammad Ali Center opened in Louisville, Kentucky, the champion's hometown. The stunning, $60 million not-for-profit center promotes peace, social responsibility, respect, and personal growth.

Also in 2005, during a ceremony at the White House, Ali received the Presidential Medal of Freedom, the nation's highest civilian award. In his remarks during the ceremony, President George W. Bush said: "This is a man who once fought more than 10 rounds with a fractured jaw. And he fought to complete exhaustion—and victory—in that legendary clash of greats in Manila. The real mystery, I guess, is how he stayed so pretty. It probably had to do with his beautiful soul. He was a fierce fighter and he's a man of peace, just like Odessa and Cassius Clay, Sr., believed their son could be. Across the world, billions of people know Muhammad Ali as a brave, compassionate, and charming man, and the American people are proud to call Muhammad Ali one of our own."

It has been quite a journey for Ali. Once, he was criticized for being divisive and arrogant. Many felt he fueled racial tensions rather than soothed them. In the second act of his life, he was extolled as charitable, peaceful, and compassionate. Whatever twists and turns the journey took, he became a complete man. Above everything else, that journey was about freedom. A freedom of expression. A freedom to achieve. A freedom to conquer—and now to unite.

Through the magic of composite film, boxing fans could see what an Ali-Rocky Marciano fight might have looked like. Marciano went 49-0 in his career, but he never faced the likes of Ali.

In bestowing the Presidential Medal of Freedom on Ali in 2005, President George W. Bush said, "Across the world, billions of people know Muhammad Ali as a brave, compassionate, and charming man."

INDEX